TAMING
YOUR
FAMILY
ZOO

TAMING YOUR FAMILY ZOO

Six Weeks to Raising a Well-Mannered Child

DONNA JONES

Revell

Grand Rapids, Michigan

© 2005 by Donna Jones

Published by Fleming H. Revell
a division of Baker Publishing Group
P.O. Box 6287, Grand Rapids, MI 49516-6287

Second printing, November 2005

Printed in the United States of America

Library of Congress Cataloging-in-Publication Data
Jones, Donna, 1961-
     Taming your family zoo : six weeks to raising a well-mannered child / Donna Jones.
          p.   cm.
     Includes bibliographical references.
     ISBN 0-8007-5948-6
     1. Etiquette for children and teenagers. 2. Child rearing—Religious aspects—Christianity. I. Title.
BJ1631.J65 2005
649′.64—dc22   2004029364

Contents

INTRODUCTION

Do you ever feel like your children are monkeys and your home is a zoo? Of course you do!

But if you're like me, you want more for your family than surviving through eighteen years of chaos. You want to encourage your child to be the best he or she can be. You want helpful information you can implement in real life. You want to raise a child who loves God and others. This book was written with you in mind.

Taming Your Family Zoo: Six Weeks to Raising a Well-Mannered Child is a practical manual that offers attainable, age-appropriate tips for raising a well-mannered child. The book is divided into two sections: Training the Trainer—You! and Training Your Child. In these pages I will walk you through the "how-to's" of developing a confident, courteous, well-mannered child. You will find many real-life stories from families just like yours. My hope is that you will find encouragement in these pages.

Taming Your Family Zoo was written for every parent who wants to *visit* the zoo, not live in it!

TRAINING THE TRAINER—YOU!

1

THERE IS HOPE!

I hate spitting.

I never dreamed that I would be spit on by a monkey—especially a monkey that was my own.

It began like a thousand other days. The springtime sun warmed my arms as my children and I happily drove to the park—another perfect day in sunny Southern California. We were to meet several friends from church, along with their children, all roughly the same ages as my three. The sound of familiar preschool melodies filled the car as we cruised to our destination.

I pulled into the closest spot available in the crowded parking lot. My children quickly spotted their playmates and squirmed excitedly as they waited for me to unbuckle first one, then two, then three car seats. The older two, as eager as two racehorses in the gate, waited as patiently as could be expected while I placed their six-month-old sister in her stroller. When I was finally ready, off they flew, across the grass and down the hill, with the kind of pure and uninhibited laughter that somehow only children can muster.

They swung, climbed, twirled, and danced. They got dirt under their nails and sand in their hair. They dined on peanut-butter sandwiches and red juice boxes. They exchanged silly knock-knock jokes and private whispers. They were in kid heaven.

Truthfully, I was in heaven too. There was not a hint of hitting, biting, or tattling among anyone's children. The other mothers and I got a few precious, uninterrupted moments to visit and laugh. And every so often one of us would jump up and swing or climb or twirl with our kids. We laughed almost as gleefully as they did. It was the perfect day—almost.

When the last juice box was empty and the last fishy cracker eaten, it was nearly time for us to head for home, so I prepared my children for our departure with the infamous "five-minute warning." You know the one.

"Kids, we have five more minutes to play," I called sweetly.

At two minutes I again reminded my children that soon it would be time to go. I gave one final reminder as "zero" hour loomed near.

At first my children ignored me. I chalked it up to being caught up in the excitement of the day, but a bit embarrassed, I walked over to my two oldest and repeated, "It's time to go now."

My three-year-old immediately grabbed my hand and prepared to go. My six-year-old was another story. First he began to whine. Next came the crying. Then the wailing. Finally, he stomped his feet in complete defiance. By this time my friends, along with every mother at the park, had stopped their conversation and become totally engrossed in our little display. I could feel every eye riveted to our scene, every mind wondering how I would handle this all-too-common scenario. We had become unwilling actors in a play whose ending was yet to be written.

What I *wanted* to do was bury myself in the sandbox. What I did instead, was try to regain control of a bad situation quickly going south.

So, with an infant-laden stroller and every sand toy known to humankind in one hand and a three-year-old child hanging on to my other arm, I somehow managed to take my son's arm and usher him toward the car. I willed my eyes to face forward, trying to ignore the other mothers' stares and my son's incessant crying.

When at last I could take it no longer, I stopped dead in my tracks, bent down to face my son squarely in the eye, and hissed under my breath, "Taylor Michael Jones, we are going home. Stop this now!"

And then he did it. The unthinkable. The unimaginable. Every mother's worst nightmare. My darling, normally well-mannered child *spit in my face*!

Eight years later . . .

It began like a thousand other days. The abrupt ring startled me out of deep thought as I reached for one dish, then two, then three . . . routinely unloading the dishwasher, relishing the quiet moments after my three children bounded out the door for school. I reached for the phone.

"Hello. Mrs. Jones?" said the unfamiliar voice.

"Yes. This is Mrs. Jones," I hesitantly replied.

"Mrs. Jones, this is Mr. Orjeron, your son, Taylor's, eighth-grade history teacher."

Uh-oh, I thought. "Y–yes . . . ," I faltered.

"Mrs. Jones, I am on my morning break grading papers. To be quite honest, I was getting very discouraged."

"Yes." *Oh no.*

"I've graded over one hundred tests, and most of the grades have been Ds or Fs."

"I see." *Great. Just great.*

"And then I came to Taylor's test."

"Yes." *Oh, Lord, what's next?*

13

"Mrs. Jones, I wanted to let you know that Taylor received a 100 percent. But that is not the real reason I'm calling."

"It's not?" *Oh, my!*

"No, Mrs. Jones, it's not. I wanted to call to let you know not only what a good job he is doing at school but, more important, what a good person you are raising."

Me, Lord? Could this be the same child who spit in my face?

"I wanted to let you know that you have a son you should be proud of. He is respectful, polite, well-mannered, and thoughtful of others. But he also has a great sense of humor and is well liked by his peers. And so, Mrs. Jones, I just wanted to take a moment out of my day to say thank you for raising a great kid."

"Thank *you*, Mr. Orjeron." *Thank you, Lord. There is hope!*

There *is* hope. Maybe your child has never done anything as disrespectful as spitting in your face, but if you are like most parents, I'll bet there has been a time or two when you've wondered, *Whose child is this, anyway?* A moment of exasperation, perhaps, or a moment of embarrassment or disbelief. A moment when you were certain you were doing things all wrong as a parent. I've been there. We've all been there. Yet there is hope! The child that baffles you now can amaze you later—if you are prepared to guide that child armed with wisdom and knowledge.

Ten years later our family laughs at Taylor's spitting episode. What once made me feel horrified and defeated now seems funny. And Taylor, at seventeen, can't believe he ever did such a thing. The point? Whether you feel you and your family need just a few pointers where courtesy is concerned or you feel your children's manners are something that could make the cover of *National Geographic*, you *can* tame your family zoo.

Of course, in today's society, it is not as simple as it once was. According to a 2002 study done by Public Agenda Research Group, nearly eight in ten respondents said "lack of respect

14

and courtesy is a serious national problem; 61% blamed parents for not instilling courtesy in their children."[1] A similar poll done by *U.S. News & World Report* found that "eight out of ten of us, both with kids and without kids, agree that bad parenting—the failure to instill good behavior in kids—is the major cause of bad manners."[2] But perhaps most shocking of all is the telephone survey done by Rasmussen Research, in which eight out of ten respondents said that "children today display worse manners than in the past, *when the respondents themselves were children*."[3] Clearly, lack of manners caused by ineffective parenting has become a serious issue in today's fast-paced society.

Raising a well-mannered child is one of the greatest gifts you can give your child—and yourself. Studies link good manners with success. Well-mannered kids have better relationships with their peers and with adults, and they are perceived more positively by others and feel more confident. Homes in which manners are practiced as part of everyday behavior are less stressful and more harmonious. And the benefit of possessing good manners doesn't end with childhood. Well-mannered adults have more success professionally and personally than their less socially adept counterparts. Instilling good manners is not only for the rich or the elite. On the contrary, good manners should be the goal of every family.

But how do you do it? In an increasingly self-centered, etiquette-illiterate culture, how do you raise a well-mannered child?

In the pages that follow, I answer that question. My purpose for writing this book is to give you hope and help in raising a child who loves God and loves others—for that is what etiquette is really all about.

Since 1988 I have taught thousands of children good manners in my children's etiquette class, Confidence & Courtesies. On the first day of class, the children learn that etiquette is "kind and considerate behavior." Etiquette is not something we reserve for company or special occasions. Etiquette does not go out of style or become irrelevant. Etiquette—good manners—is something to be used every day and with everyone. Good manners are to be used at home, at school, in restaurants and stores—everywhere.

They are to be part of the way we relate to parents, siblings, teachers, and friends. Jesus taught us to "do to others as you would have them do to you" (Luke 6:31). This admonition is the basis for etiquette. Etiquette is not about being "hoity-toity," as my children like to say. No, etiquette is quite the opposite. Etiquette is about humility, unselfishness, and respect. Etiquette involves treating others as you wish to be treated.

And when you have a home filled with people who live like this, you have a home that is a safe haven, a sanctuary, a secure refuge.

Good Parents "Parent"

But I live in the real world. I have real children. Sometimes the peaceful haven I long for feels more like the local zoo at feeding time. Can you relate? As much as we love our little monkeys, they can wreak havoc on our idealistic notions of blissful family life.

I have never felt more out of control of my three little "monkeys" than on that fateful day at the park ten years ago. I questioned my parenting methods, style, and ability. Fortunately, my temporary defeat didn't lead to despair. Why? Because I knew then and know now, two key facts:

- Children are a work in process.
- Good parents "parent."

What does this mean? In simple terms it means that no child is perfect. Children are not miniature adults. Children are children. They are in the process of learning appropriate and inappropriate behavior. They are bound to make mistakes or poor choices along the way. It is our job to teach them to make the right choices.

Many parents unwisely and naively feel inadequate as parents simply because their child misbehaves. But we can learn to see our child's misbehavior not as a failure but as an opportunity. Each time a child chooses an inappropriate behavior, we can seize that opportunity as a teachable moment—a moment to instruct, encourage, or discipline. When we see our child's behavior through the grid of "teachable moments," we are freed from the unrealistic desire to be perfect parents with perfect children. Instead, we can become wise parents who are in the process of raising healthy, happy, well-behaved children.

When my friends Rex and Andrea Minor, both now on staff at Willow Creek Community Church, had young children, their daughter Paige became unruly while sitting with them during an adult Sunday school class on—of all things—parenting. After trying unsuccessfully to calm her once, Rex lifted an irritable, inconsolable two-year-old Paige into his arms and quickly left the room. Later, on their way home, Andrea commented on how embarrassed she felt over little Paige's behavior.

> *We should never be embarrassed that our child misbehaves. We should only be embarrassed if we fail to deal with our child's misbehavior.*

"Andrea," Rex responded, "we should never be embarrassed that our child misbehaves. *We should only be embarrassed if we fail to deal with our child's misbehavior.*"

I would be willing to bet, however, that you, like me, have felt embarrassed over your child's behavior at one time or another. Why? Because somewhere in the deep recesses of our minds, we believe that if we were the kind of parents we should be, our children would never misbehave. We have bought into the false notion that we can somehow be perfect parents who raise perfect children. And what happens when our children behave like children? We end up frustrated, discouraged, angry, or defeated.

Our goal is not perfection. It can't be, for we will never be perfect this side of heaven, nor will our children. No, our goal is wisdom—wisdom to raise children who love God and others.

When asked, "Which is the greatest commandment in the Law?" Jesus responded, "Love the Lord your God with all your heart and with all your soul and with all your mind." But he didn't stop there. He went on to add, "And the second is like it: 'Love your neighbor as yourself'" (Matt. 22:36–39). The good manners we teach our children are based on these two commandments. Our job is to wisely instill these principles into our children.

Sixteen years have come and gone since Paige Minor squirmed her way out of the third row at church; eleven years have passed since my son, Taylor's, spitting spree. Now well into their teens, both kids are confident and courteous young adults who are a source of joy to their family and friends. Their character development didn't happen overnight. But it did happen. And it can happen for your child too.

Children are a work in progress, but armed with knowledge, perseverance, and wisdom, you can help your child embrace good manners as a way of life. Doing so will increase confidence and decrease chaos. It will lighten tension and heighten peace. Now who wouldn't want a home like that?

2

THE FIRST ABSOLUTELY, POSITIVELY ESSENTIAL PRINCIPLE FOR TAMING YOUR FAMILY ZOO

He was certain he knew the cardinal rule of raising a teenage boy: "No public signs of affection."

A room filled with hormonal teenage boys in the middle of a rigorous after-school wrestling practice is no place for the faint of heart—or nose. But my husband had prepared himself to be insensitive to the offensive odors wafting from the practice gym of our son's high school. Yes, he could ignore the odor. But no amount of preparation could have made him insensitive to what was about to transpire.

My husband, J.P., watched silently as the young men wrestled on the mat, each attempting to claim their place as the dominant male. They grunted and grappled as their coach called out direction and help from the sideline.

Not wanting to intrude, J.P. discretely approached our son to quickly ask what time practice would end. After learning that the boys still had another hour of practice, J.P. decided to leave and return later. As J.P. turned to go, he consciously stopped himself from calling out his usual departing "I love you" to our son.

Our six-feet-tall, then fifteen-year-old son's words were not so measured.

"Bye, Dad. I love you," he called without thinking.

The silence that followed made my husband and son cringe.

Finally, one hulking boy broke the silence. "Aw, Taylor loves his daddy," he teased.

My husband could only hope that the ridicule wouldn't be too harsh, too embarrassing.

But then the unbelievable occurred. Something you don't read about in the newspapers or hear about on TV—something you might never expect from a bunch of public high school jocks.

Without hesitation one of the other boys called from across the gym, "Hey, I love my dad too."

"Yeah, me too," added another.

One kid actually stopped wrestling, stood up, and declared, "Hey, I love my mom *and* my dad."

My husband's heart melted.

Go figure. Even teenagers know it's cool for parents and kids to love each other.

Quite obviously (and to our amazement!) this group of teenage boys had grasped the first of the two absolutely, positively essential principles for raising a happy, healthy, well-behaved child—love.

Creating an Environment of Love

Nothing compares to love when it comes to taming a family zoo. All the etiquette skills and manners lessons in the world will not create a happy home or a happy child apart from love. A home filled with love is crucial.

If I were to poll parents with the question, "Do you love your child?" no doubt the results overwhelmingly would be "Yes!" Yet not every child feels loved. Not every child experiences the confidence of parental love my son's teammates had experienced. Not every child reaches adulthood fully secure in the love of his or her mother and father.

Why not? If most parents love their children, why do many children grow up doubting that love? Why do some adults still long for the love of their parents? Still hope for it? Still try to perform for it?

More important, what can we do to ensure that our children grow up secure in our love? The answer lies in the nature of love—in what love *really* is and in how love is communicated in our homes.

Contrary to popular notion, love is not a feeling. Love is action—sacrificial, others-centered, unconditional action. And whether or not we grow up secure in love is based in large part on the actions of those around us, especially our parents.

Love Is Unconditional and Others-Centered

"Mom, I'm not going!" she declared.

This was going to be another long day.

"Why not?" I asked, trying my best to understand.

"Because I can't do the dive and I don't want to blow it in front of all those people. That's why."

"Honey, I'm sure you can do it. Your coach believes you can. And, sweetheart, if you just try, in our eyes you'll be a winner."

It was a good thing I added the last part.

My daughter was competing in her first Junior Olympic dive meet, and she was scared to death. It was a warm June day, and the stands were packed. I felt confident in her ability until I actually witnessed the dive she had warned me about.

Uh-oh, I thought as I watched her warm up.

Actually, all went well up until it was time for the dreaded dive. Towering three meters in the air, my petite fifth grader reached the end of the board and jumped.

It certainly wasn't the best dive of the day, and it wasn't going to earn her any medals, but we clapped and shouted and cheered anyway. When her ten-year-old freckled face popped up out of the water, her eyes turned to meet our gaze. We smiled and gave her two thumbs up. Her broad grin reached from ear to ear.

We were thrilled. She had tried her best.

The next diver, ten-year-old Brittany, was to perform the same dive as our daughter. During warm-up earlier that morning, we watched as she flawlessly practiced it again and again. Now she walked ever so slowly to the end of the towering board. She paused, focusing. At least that's what we thought she was doing. All the best divers did it.

Except then Brittany's face began to show signs that looked less like focus and more like fear. Brittany stood atop the board, not moving even the slightest muscle. Five seconds turned into ten. The tension began to grow. Pity, embarrassment, and discomfort filled the air. No one had ever seen a diver do this. Ten seconds turned into twenty.

Finally, someone in the massive crowd yelled, "You can do it, Brittany."

"Go for it, Brittany," called another.

In exasperation, Brittany's parents yelled, "Jump Brittany. Just jump!"

Twenty seconds turned into thirty, and still Brittany remained frozen.

Then came the words everyone dreaded.

"Failed dive," the judge pronounced. "Diver, please step down from the board," the announcer declared clear and strong for all to hear.

So, with all eyes watching, little Brittany, embarrassed from failure, turned, descended the steps, and faced defeat. Humiliated, Brittany walked head-down toward what surely would be the comfort of her mother and father.

We were seated only a few feet away from Brittany's parents, so we tried to avert our eyes when Brittany reached her mom and dad, trying desperately to hold back the onslaught of tears.

Our children do not exist to nurture us; we exist to nurture our children.

"Don't you dare cry," Brittany's father hissed.

Brittany sniffled, trying her best to hold her emotions in check, though not doing a very good job.

"I mean it, Brittany," we heard him harshly repeat under his breath. "*Don't cry.*"

She was just a ten-year-old child—a heartbroken, defeated, embarrassed ten-year-old child. What she needed was comfort, encouragement, acceptance, and love. She never got it.

What was wrong with this dad? Didn't he love his daughter? Almost certainly he would *say* he did. So why did he act that way?

Because he failed to realize that love—real love—is unconditional and others-centered. Love is about what your child needs, not about what you need. Love is about building up your child, not your child somehow building up you.

This dad, like so many parents, looked to his child's performance to make him feel good, to fill *his* cup, so to speak. He equated Brittany's failure with his failure. So when Brittany failed to perform, his acceptance was withdrawn.

We don't have children to fill our gaps. Our children are not responsible for helping us feel good, healing our marriage, or feeding our egos. Our children do not exist to nurture us; we exist to nurture our children. This may seem obvious, but the opposite scenario plays itself out every day in homes across the country.

Though we may never face what Brittany and her father faced, the temptation to be a self-centered parent who accepts his child conditionally still subtly lures us. Ask yourself whether you have ever pressured your child to perform athletically, academically, socially, or spiritually in order to "keep up" or "be better than" other kids.

Maybe your Johnny isn't walking as early or reading as well as your best friend's child. Or maybe he doesn't hit homers or make straight A's like that child. And so you feel pressure to "help" him perform to some arbitrary standard: walk by ten months, read by four years, make the most goals, get invited to the most parties, make the best grades, memorize the most Scripture, or even have the best manners. Why? Is it really for your child? Or is all the pressure you place on your child really for you?

Love isn't about us parents. Love is about our children. What is best for our children? What, at this moment, do our children need? As the Bible so aptly puts it, "Each of you should look not only to your own interests, but also the interests of others" (Phil. 2:4).

Look at your child with the eyes of your heart.

Sometimes, as in Brittany's case, love means unconditional acceptance. It means that your child is *certain* that you will love and accept her when she is first in the class or when she is last; when he is the best on the team or when he is the worst; when she succeeds or when she fails.

Often I hear my mother's words of wisdom ringing in my ears: "Look at your child with the eyes of your heart." To know what our children need, we must look not only at their actions, but at their souls.

Love Involves Limits

Real love means unconditional acceptance. But real love also involves limits. This important aspect of love is perhaps the

24

most misunderstood component of real love. Many parents mistakenly believe that love is an ooey, gooey, anything-goes feeling. Nothing could be further from the truth. To feel truly loved and secure, a child needs boundaries and discipline. But, out of fear of being labeled "mean," "unloving," or even "abusive," many parents loosen limits and discard discipline the minute their little monkeys show the first signs of displeasure.

Of course children will complain when we require chores, completed homework, or thank you notes. But just because our children complain doesn't mean we are acting as unloving parents. In fact, the opposite may be true. Consider this insightful essay:

Was your mom mean?

I know mine was. We had the meanest mother in the whole world!

While other kids ate candy for breakfast, we had to have cereal, eggs, and toast.

When others had a Pepsi and a Twinkie for lunch, we had to eat sandwiches.

And you can guess our mother fixed us a dinner that was different from what other kids had, too.

Mother insisted on knowing where we were at all times.

You'd think we were convicts in a prison.

She had to know who our friends were and what we were doing with them.

She insisted that if we said we would be gone for an hour, we would be gone for an hour or less.

We were ashamed to admit it, but she had the nerve to break the child labor laws by making us work.

We had to wash the dishes, make the beds, learn to cook, vacuum the floor, do laundry, empty the trash and all sorts of cruel jobs.

I think she would lie awake at night thinking of more things for us to do.

She always insisted on us telling the truth, the whole truth, and nothing but the truth.

By the time we were teenagers, she could read our minds.
Then life was really tough!
Mother wouldn't let our friends just honk the horn when they
drove up. They had to come up to the door so she could
meet them.
While everyone else could date when they were twelve or thir-
teen, we had to wait until we were sixteen.
Because of our mother, we missed out on lots of things other
kids experienced.
None of us has ever been caught shoplifting or vandalizing
others' property or been arrested for any crime.
It was all her fault.
Now that we have left home, we are all educated, honest adults.
We are doing our best to be mean parents just like Mom was.
I think that is what's wrong with the world today.
It just doesn't have enough mean moms!

Author Unknown

Inevitably, parents who set limits have those limits tested
and questioned. "Mean" moms and dads can expect to hear
"Why can't I?" and "How come?" over and over again. I
believe the best answer is not "Because I said so" but rather,
"Because I love you." Loving parents set limits because they
care.

Loving parents remain consistent no matter how un-
popular the limits, because loving parents act in the best
interests of their child. Security comes from knowing the
boundaries and being able to count on those boundaries
remaining constant.

The most insecure children in the world are those whose
parents have failed to set consistent boundaries.

Setting Limits

How does a loving parent set limits? By making boundaries clear, consistent, and reasonable.

Both parent and child become frustrated when limits are unclear. Rules should be few yet unmistakable. Simple clarity makes it easy for a child to discern obedience from disobedience. When rules are too complex or too numerous, a child is bound to fail. When setting limits, focus on the majors, and the minors will generally take care of themselves. Non-negotiable limits might include "Obey parents the first time" and "No hitting, name calling, or other hurtful behaviors." These rules are uncomplicated and applicable to children and teens as well. If a child hits his sister, he knows without a doubt his behavior was unacceptable. Make your child's limits unmistakable, unambiguous, and uncomplicated. Make your limits clear.

In addition, enforce your limits with consistency. To feel secure, children need to know the limits, and they also need to know that the limits will be enforced. It does more harm than good when you set rules in place only to disregard them yourself. Children can feel secure only if they know what the boundary lines are and that the boundary lines will not be moved. The bottom line is this: If you say it, do it! Be a parent of your word. Without consistency children cannot feel the security of parental love.

When setting limits, focus on the majors, and the minors will generally take care of themselves.

Finally, limits must be reasonable. Family rules and limits will differ depending on your child's age and maturity level. A two-year-old cannot and should not be expected to behave in ways suitable for a six-year-old. A teenager will need to be given more freedom than a ten-year-old. Loving limits will grow and change with the maturity of your child. But to be effective, limits must always be clear, consistent, and reasonable.

Love Involves Affection

She grew up in a home where the words "I love you" were not often, if ever, spoken. Sure, she knew she was loved. She had clean clothes, food on the table, two parents at home. But still she longed to hear the words. So she made herself a promise. When she had children, she would make sure they knew they were loved. She would tell them. She would show them. She would hug, kiss, and hold them. They would never doubt. They would know.

She grew up, had three children of her own, and kept her promise. Not a day went by that she failed to tell her children that they were loved. She is my mother.

What does it do for a child to hear the words "I love you"? I can tell you from firsthand experience that these three simple words can create a sense of security like no other. Children need to know they are loved. They need to see it and hear it. The power of the words "I love you" affects not only your child, but the atmosphere of your home as well. It's impossible to tame your family zoo without first creating an atmosphere of love in your home. Love smoothes rough edges and softens cold hearts. Love covers a multitude of sins. It's hard for tension to reign, even among siblings, when love fills a home. Of course, even in the most loving homes, siblings sometimes quarrel. Still, when love pervades the atmosphere of a home—when each member feels loved, cared for, and valued—brothers and sisters will hug, not just hit; they will cooperate, not merely compete; they will talk with one another, not simply ignore. Love unifies. Love binds. Love never fails.

Speaking the words comes easier for some people than for others, but saying, "I love you," can be simple. Try saying, "I love you," before you leave your child's room at night, before he leaves for school, or before he hangs up the phone. Even if saying, "I love you," seems awkward, say it anyway. Life is too short and your child is too precious to leave these important words unspoken.

Loving words must be backed up with loving actions. An environment of love cannot be created with mere words alone. Affection is vital. Hugging, kissing, patting, hair tousling, wrestling, playing—these actions are necessary for a child to experience the security of love we all long for.

Frequently when a child acts out, she is simply, almost primitively, crying out for attention and affection. When my children were young, I often understood patterns of unusual "acting out" as signs that my child needed a bit more attention. So I made a special effort to place that child on my lap, read a book with my child, or just sit and talk. Our older children and teens often benefit from fun one-on-one time with their father or me. In almost every instance, these acts of affection stilled my child's cry for attention and the negative behavior disappeared.

Love Involves Forgiveness

"I'm sorry. Would you forgive Mommy for yelling today?" the tired young mom asked her daughter as she tucked the older of her two preschool-age children into bed after a long, hard day. She sat down beside her daughter and began to stroke her hair.

"Oh, Mom, don't worry. We'd miss it if you didn't yell some-times," her four-year-old replied nonchalantly.

Every parent blows it. Every child blows it. Hence, the need for the words "I'm sorry," "I was wrong," and "Would you forgive me?"

Are these weak words? Unnecessary words? Words that admit failure or perhaps deficiency?

No, these words are heard regularly in homes filled with love. Why? Because a vital part of love is forgiveness.

Loving homes are not perfect homes. Children from loving homes sometimes whine, cry, or disobey. Parents in loving homes sometimes yell or handle things in ways they regret.

Loving families deal with the same issues every family deals with. What makes a loving home loving is the presence of forgiveness.

How do you and I create an environment of loving forgiveness? We live it.

I often observe parents teaching their small children to say, "I'm sorry," when they hit, bite, or grab a toy. While this is a commendable first step in creating an environment of forgiveness, it is equally important for parents to say, "I'm sorry."

Apologizing to our children when we make mistakes takes humility. Extending forgiveness to our children when they make mistakes takes compassion. Together they form a bond of love. As the Bible so aptly puts it, "Love covers over a multitude of sins" (1 Peter 4:8).

> *Apologizing to our children when we make mistakes takes humility. Extending forgiveness to our children when they make mistakes takes compassion. Together they form a bond of love.*

Jesus told his disciples, "A new command I give you: Love one another. As I have loved you, so you must love one another" (John 13:34). How does Jesus love us? With *complete* forgiveness.

The mother or father who seeks their child's forgiveness models the honesty, integrity, and humility it takes to make relationships work. The child who witnesses this kind of parental maturity is fortunate to get a firsthand view of love in action. By the same token, a child who is granted forgiveness experiences mercy and grace. "I'll love you if . . ." isn't love at all. "I love you *even* if . . ." is the type of love Christ modeled on the cross and the type of love he calls us to extend to others.

I recall a particularly difficult day when I was a teenager. Everything had gone wrong. So, like most teenagers, I took

30

all my frustration out on my mother. I was crabby, sassy, and downright rotten. My mother would have been well within her rights to punish me for such disrespectful behavior. And under normal circumstances she might have. But this day she didn't.

Sensing my anguish, she responded with nothing but kindness.

"Mom, why have you been so nice to me when I've been such a brat all day long?" I remember asking her.

"Because, honey, I know how you feel. And sometimes we all need to know we're loved no matter what."

Creating an atmosphere of love by unconditionally accepting your child, setting limits, showing affection, and practicing forgiveness won't mean life will be trouble-free. Your kids will still have good days and bad, up days and down, successes and failures. And so will you. Creating a home filled with love won't make life perfect, but it will make it secure. The issues you face may be no different from those of your neighbor. The difference, however, will reside in the peace, joy, and security that pervade the hearts and minds of the blessed family members who live in a loving home.

I Loved You Enough . . .

Someday when my children are old enough to understand the logic that motivates a parent, I will tell them:

I loved you enough . . . to ask where you were going, with whom, and what time you would be home.

I loved you enough . . . to insist that you save your money and buy a bike for yourself even though we could afford to buy one for you.

I loved you enough . . . to be silent and let you discover that your new best friend was a creep.

I loved you enough . . . to make you go pay for the bubble gum you had taken and tell the clerk, "I stole this yesterday and want to pay for it."

31

I loved you enough . . . to stand over you for two hours while you cleaned your room, a job that should have taken fifteen minutes.

I loved you enough . . . to let you see anger, disappointment, and tears in my eyes. Children must learn that their parents aren't perfect.

I loved you enough . . . to let you assume the responsibility for your actions even when the penalties were so harsh they almost broke my heart.

But most of all, I loved you enough . . . to say *no* when I knew you would hate me for it. Those were the most difficult battles of all. I'm glad I won them, because in the end you won too.

And someday when your children are old enough to understand the logic that motivates parents, you will tell them

I loved you enough . . .

Author Unknown

Practical Tips for Creating a Loving Home

1. Say, "I love you," every day.
2. Pray for your child—and let your child hear.
3. Hug, kiss, hold, wrestle with, and play with your child.
4. Spend time with your child.
5. Look at your child when your child speaks to you.
6. Smile at your child.
7. Love your child's father or mother.
8. Accept your child's God-given uniqueness.
9. Tell your child, "I like you."
10. Set limits and stick to them.

3

THE SECOND ABSOLUTELY, POSITIVELY ESSENTIAL PRINCIPLE FOR TAMING YOUR FAMILY ZOO

Tired. Overwhelmed. Exhausted. That's what I thought when I saw her for the first time.

It didn't take me long to figure out why. Her two-year-old daughter sat perched on her lap as we chatted. Our conversation lasted only a minute or two before her child began to playfully smack her in the face.

"No, Claire. Don't hit Mommy."

Claire stopped for about thirty nanoseconds before she swatted her mother again, this time a bit harder.

"Claire, please don't hit Mommy. It's not nice."

After Claire's fourth swat at her mother's face, she became bored with the game she knew she could win. She hopped off her mother's lap. Her mother breathed a sigh of relief, her countenance visibly lightened.

A few moments later, Claire finagled her way onto her uncle's lap. When Claire slapped his face, we all smiled in embarrassment while her mother offered a lame apology.

This mother unwittingly allowed herself to be treated disrespectfully. By refusing to effectively deal with Claire's behavior, she granted Claire permission to treat her with contempt. The result? At the age of two, Claire not only treated her mother disrespectfully but other adults as well. No wonder her mother looked stressed out.

The Necessity of Respect in a Happy Home

Next to loving your kids, instilling respect is the most important task you have as a parent.

Children who are "loved" but not taught the importance of respect for those around them are really not loved at all. They are simply spoiled.

Respect is as essential to creating a happy home and taming your family zoo as is love. The two go hand in hand. In fact, real love cannot exist apart from respect. Children who are "loved" but not taught the importance of respect for those around them are really not loved at all. They are simply spoiled.

Respect is defined as "to listen to, to heed, to hold in high regard, to esteem." Is it any wonder then that respect is the second essential principle for taming your family zoo? It is imperative for children to learn to respect parents, adults, peers, siblings, and even things.

Respect Is God's Idea

Respect is the basis for Jesus's command, "Do to others as you would have them do to you" (Luke 6:31). When we hold other people in high regard, we treat them as we wish to be treated because we understand that other people have value. Respect is the antithesis of selfish, self-centered living.

Respect is also the basis for etiquette. Etiquette is "kind and considerate behavior"—the very essence of respect. When you teach your children manners, you teach them respect.

The idea of respect in the family goes back at least as far as Moses. God places such a high value on respect in the home that he included it in the Ten Commandments. "Honor your father and your mother" is the fifth commandment (Exod. 20:12), and it is the first commandment with a promise.

The reality of this promise has a profound impact on the happiness and emotional health of our homes. This command and promise is repeated by the apostle Paul: "Honor your father and mother . . . that it may go well with you and that you may enjoy long life on the earth" (Eph. 6:2–3).

Did you catch that promise? Why should we honor our parents and teach our children to honor us? So that it may go well with us and we may enjoy long life on the earth. Having a life that goes well and is enjoyable is intricately tied up with the issue of respect. In short, if respect is present in a home, happiness is able to flourish. If respect is absent, happiness and peace cannot thrive.

Respectful Kids = Happy Home

He looked about sixteen. He waved a fifty-dollar sweatshirt in front of his mother's face, much like a two-year-old with a desired toy. Complete disdain and disregard filled his eyes as I overheard his mother quietly whisper, "I can't afford it right now, Justin. If you want it, you'll need to buy it with your allowance."

"You *will* buy it for me, you b——."

Terror filled her eyes. She pulled out her wallet and bought the sweatshirt.

The dark-haired, brown-eyed girl with a silky-smooth olive complexion looked about eleven or twelve. I overheard her comment just an hour or so after I had witnessed Justin's disrespectful threat to his mother.

As the girl's mother bent over the counter, carefully writing a check for her daughter's new shoes, I heard her daughter sweetly whisper, "Thanks, Mom." Their eyes met as both smiled.

So, whose home is happier? You don't have to be a genius, parenting expert, or Ph.D. to figure out that homes in which children are taught to respect others are happier and healthier than homes in which children are not taught the value of respect.

To raise a happy, emotionally healthy, well-mannered child, both love and respect are essential.

Teaching Children to Respect Their Parents

The necessity of respect has somehow become lost in our culture. Many children talk to their parents, teachers, and coaches as if they are peers. Other children are allowed to decide whether they want to obey their parents or teachers. Many more are permitted to engage in behaviors that infringe on the rights of others. Should we be surprised, then, that our homes, classrooms, and playgrounds have become chaotic? We *know* something is lacking in today's society. The missing character quality is respect. The smooth functioning of a home, a business, a school, or a society depends on it.

So where do we begin? Respect begins with the parents. It is essential for children to respect their mothers and fathers. Respect for parents is both a right and a privilege.

Children should be *expected* to treat parents respectfully. The respect we receive because we are a child's mother or father does not need to be earned—it is required simply because of our position. In other words, a child needs to learn to treat people in authority—beginning with his parents—respectfully.

Being treated respectfully is the right of every parent. We do not have to apologize or feel guilty when we require our children to treat us with respect. We do our children no favors when we allow them to use disrespectful words, actions, or tone of voice. For parents who desire to tame their family zoo, respect is nonnegotiable.

> *It might be easy to say, "Do as I say, not as I do," but it sure won't earn you your child's respect.*

Although respect is the right of every parent, it is also a privilege. You can require your child to treat you respectfully, but your child will never respect you if you don't live a life worthy of respect.

Little Eyes Are Watching

So, how are you doing in the honesty department? Do you live a life of integrity? How about your words? Do you gossip, use foul language, or criticize others? What about your schedule? Do you make time to spend with your child? Are you modeling an authentic relationship with God? Are you humble? Do you ask for forgiveness when you blow it? Are you kind? How about patient? Are you self-controlled? These qualities, among others, exemplify a life worth following. It might be easy to say, "Do as I say, not as I do," but it sure won't earn you your child's respect.

Little Eyes upon You

There are little eyes upon you
and they're watching night and day.
There are little ears that quickly
take in every word you say.

There are little hands all eager
to do anything you do;
and a little boy who's dreaming
of the day he'll be like you.
You're the little fellow's idol,
you're the wisest of the wise.
In his little mind about you
no suspicions ever rise.
He believes in you devoutly,
holds all you say and do;
he will say and do, in your way
when he's grown up just like you.
There's a wide-eyed little fellow
who believes you're always right;
and his eyes are always opened,
and he watches day and night.
You are setting an example
every day in all you do;
for the little boy who's waiting
to grow up to be like you.

Author Unknown

Raising a Respectful Child

Fortunately, imparting a few basic manners can help instill respect into the heart of your child. Teach your child to address adults as Mr., Mrs., or Miss, for example. In our increasingly casual culture, where the lines separating adults and children have become blurred, this simple courtesy has largely gone by the wayside. Many adults feel uncomfortable having friends' children address them as Mr. or Mrs. To many of our ears, those terms sound old, as if they belong to our parents, not us. So we invite children to call us by our first names, not realizing that being on a first-name basis invites familiarity and a sense of equality that can hinder healthy, normal respect children need to have for adults.

If being addressed by your last name seems too formal for you, then at least consider having children use Mr., Mrs., or Miss before your first name. "Miss Kathy" or "Mr. Bob" can be a friendly alternative that still communicates respect.

Other manners, which will be covered more extensively in later chapters, also teach the importance of respect with adults. For instance:

- Children stand when introduced to an adult.
- Children respond when adults speak to them.
- Children offer their seats to adults.
- Children do not interrupt adult conversations.

An Obedient Kid Is a Respectful Kid

Perhaps the most important job we parents have in creating a respectful child is to teach our children to obey. Willful disobedience is not simply childish behavior, but blatant disregard for a parent's instructions. Willful disobedience is the embodiment of disrespect.

When a child digs in her little heels, looks you in the eye, and says no, she is not merely asserting her independence as some experts would have us believe. No, a child who refuses to comply—whether actively or passively—is asking the questions, "Who's in charge?" "Where are the boundaries?" and "Will you lead me in such a way that I will respect you?" How a parent responds in moments of defiance determines the relationship between parent and child. If the parent leads with firm and loving discipline, the result will be a secure, respectful child.

In his book *The New Dare to Discipline*, Dr. James Dobson notes:

When properly applied, loving discipline works! It stimulates tender affection, made possible by *mutual* respect between a parent and a child. It bridges the gap which otherwise separates family members who should love and trust each other. It allows the God of our ancestors to be introduced to our beloved children. It permits teachers to do the kind of job in the classroom for which they were commissioned. It encourages a child to respect other people and live as a responsible, constructive citizen.[1]

The same biblical passage that teaches the importance of respect in the home also offers this instruction: "Children, obey your parents in the Lord, for this is right. 'Honor your father and mother' . . . 'that it may go well with you and that you may live long on the earth'" (Eph. 6:1–3). To have a happy home, children must learn to obey their parents.

Teaching our children to obey is a parent's responsibility. The Ephesians passage continues, "Fathers, do not exasperate your children; instead, bring them up in the training and instruction of the Lord" (Eph. 6:4). In teaching our kids to obey, we are not to exasperate them. We are not to aggravate, irritate, or provoke them. Our job is to lovingly teach and train them to do right.

One of the most helpful tips I learned as a young mom was to teach my children to be what I like to call, "OK kids." When OK kids are asked to do something, they don't respond with, "Just a minute" or "Why?" or "Do I have to?" or "No," but with "OK."

We practiced and rehearsed this principle using a variety of different scenarios. With our toddlers, my husband and I made a game of learning to say, "OK." The idea behind this simple, somewhat silly scene was to demonstrate obedience in a fun, nonstressful, clear way.

One of us would place ourselves at the far side of our family room. The other would sit on the sofa and say, "Come here, Daddy (or Mommy)." The standing parent would respond with "OK" while walking toward the seated parent. We cheered as the "obedient" parent walked across the room toward the sofa.

Next we included our toddler in the "OK" game, holding his or her hand as we walked toward the parent who had asked us to "come here." Once we knew our toddler understood the "game," we placed her at the far side of the room, called, "Come here," then hooted and hollered as our child toddled to us. (Remember, we are talking about an eighteen-month to three-year-old here!)

Why did we go to so much trouble just to teach our children to obey? Because children who obey their parents in the small things will also obey their parents in the big things.

During our kids' preschool years, we tried to make obeying Mom and Dad fun by having our children say, "I hear and obey," using a robot's voice. Silly? Definitely! But preschoolers love silly. They got a kick out of this goofy routine, and we got obedience. Now that our children are older, we teasingly, but nonetheless seriously, remind them, "The correct response would be 'OK, Mom (or Dad).' " Admittedly, they sometimes look at us like we live on Mars, but they know that "No" is never an option.

Whether our children were fifteen months or fifteen years old, the idea behind our methodology has been to help them make the link between obedience and blessing. Obedience is a positive not a negative.

Of course, teaching your child to be an OK kid doesn't mean that your kids can never offer their opinion, ask for more time, or give you information you weren't aware of. OK kids know that their parents are not tyrannical dictators out to make their lives miserable, but rather loving parents who expect their kids to obey for their own best interest.

In addition to teaching your child to be an OK kid, try utilizing "do overs." Let's say your child is running through the house, which she knows she is not to do. Instead of punishing your child for running, instruct her to go back and "do it over" until she walks instead of runs. A "do over" can also be effectively used when a child speaks rudely ("You need to say that again with a respectful tone of voice"), fails to complete a task ("Turn the television off, go back, and finish cleaning your room"), or in any number of situations. Sometimes parents punish their child when the real desire is for their child to behave correctly. A "do over" can be an effective tool in training our children to do what is right.

Respect in Word and Deed

If respect is seen through a child's actions, then respect is heard through a child's words.

The next time you find yourself in a public place, listen to the way children speak to their parents. Observe their words. Pay attention to their tone. If you're like me, you are bound to notice a deficit in the way many children are allowed to speak to adults.

These children speak disrespectfully because they are wrongfully allowed to do so. Would you consider speaking to your boss the way some kids speak to their teachers? Would you use the kind of language at the grocery store that some children use on the playground?

What we say and how we say it communicates respect, or lack of respect, every bit as much as obedience or disobedience. To raise a respectful child, direct your child's words as well as her actions. Directing your child's words may be as simple as saying "Please don't speak to me in that tone of voice." It might mean guarding what she watches on TV, video, or DVD. Child characters on television and in movies often do not exhibit polite, respectful behavior toward adults. Monitor the kind of role models, both real and fictional, your child sees.

Finally, the best way to raise a child who speaks respectfully is to speak respectfully yourself. Homes where moms and dads say "please" and "thank you" and speak kindly to each other and their children will generally produce kids who speak politely as well.

Respect for Your Child

Respect in the home is not reserved only for parents; children must be treated with respect as well. Children who are treated with respect develop self-confidence and security. They learn to assert themselves in positive, constructive ways. They develop healthy boundaries. They acquire inner strength. Respect is vital to developing both your child's character and emotional health.

How can parents exhibit respect for their children?

- by listening when the child speaks
- by allowing the child to make age-appropriate choices
- by never demeaning or embarrassing the child
- by being considerate of the child's needs
- by validating the child's feelings
- by allowing the child to have personal space and things
- by understanding the child's emotions
- by giving the child permission to voice personal opinions and concerns

A child raised in an environment of acceptance and respect will become a confident, secure person who treats others with respect as well. Consider the following incident.

A mother related an occurrence involving her little boy's visit to the doctor. At one point the doctor wanted to examine the boy's genitals and ordered the boy to take off his underwear.

"No. That's private. I'm not going to let you look there," the boy informed him.

The doctor snapped impatiently, "I'm sure it's OK with your mother, so take off your underwear."

The mother, though quite unimpressed with the doctor's manner, assured her son that this exam was appropriate.

"OK," the son said. Then he turned to the doctor and said in a far more polite tone than the doctor had used, "But you should have asked permission first, you know. You didn't respect me."[2]

Clearly this self-confident youngster had been raised by a mother who treated him with respect. How do I know? This child understood the difference between being treated respectfully and being treated disrespectfully. He valued his own instincts. He had internalized a sense of appropriate versus inappropriate boundaries. And he knew how to communicate his thoughts, feelings, and opinions without being disrespectful. A child treated as a valuable human being, worthy of respect, develops the confidence to assert himself in positive, constructive ways.

Respecting Siblings

When it comes to sibling relationships, one thing is certain: siblings *will* have conflict. However, how much and how intense the conflict depends in large part on how respect for others is lived out in the home. Respect between siblings creates a peaceful, harmonious environment.

A few simple, nonnegotiable rules can help tame your family zoo by creating an atmosphere of respect.

- No hitting or biting.
- No name calling.
- No using personal items (toys, CDs, books, brushes, clothes, games, etc.) without permission.

Just as we must expect respectful behavior toward adults, we must require respectful behavior between siblings.

Respecting Others

I recently attended a religious ceremony held at a home. What should have been a profoundly meaningful experience was marred by a ten-year-old boy. While the pastor eloquently explained the ceremony about to transpire, this child wandered aimlessly around the guests. At one point he began circling the host's pool. I watched as each guest, one by one, turned their attention away from the pastor's heartfelt words and toward the undisciplined child.

Parents must regain control and replace chaos with order. Happy, healthy, well-behaved children are not allowed to behave without restraint when others are involved.

Interestingly, several other children also attended this event. Though some were older and some younger than the ten-year-old tyrant, all sat quietly while the pastor spoke. Yes, children will be children, but children can be taught to behave respectfully in public venues. Teaching a child respect for others is essential to taming your family zoo.

Respecting Things

CRASH! came the sound from my living room. I ran into the pristine room just in time to see the baseball lying on the carpet, glass strewn around the floor, and a glimpse of a brown-haired boy in a red sweatshirt retreating down our street.

I waited patiently for the young culprit to return to the scene of the crime. I laughed to myself as I imagined his face when the wayward ball came crashing through our picture window. I knew he thought I would be angry. I wasn't.

But as time passed, I did wonder how I should handle the situation. Fortunately, I didn't have to wait too long. Later that evening my doorbell rang. Standing on the front porch was the young offender, his father by his side.

"Um . . . Hi, Mrs. Jones. I kinda, sorta broke your window with my baseball this afternoon. My dad and I were wondering if we could have it fixed."

This young man didn't realize it at the time, but he learned a valuable lesson that day. He learned to respect things. It's important for a child to grasp the concept that things, both others' and his own, should be treated with care. By requiring his son to replace the broken window, this wise father instilled in him a sense of respect for personal property.

This principle applies to animals and nature as well. Simple acts such as requiring a child to treat pets responsibly or forbidding a child to leave her trash at the park teach respect for all living things.

To raise a happy child, to have a happy home, to tame a family zoo, respect is crucial.

Practical Tips for Raising a Respectful Child

1. Teach your child to be an "OK kid."
2. Expect your child to treat you and other adults with respect.
3. Live a life of integrity.
4. Teach your child to address adults as Mr., Mrs., Miss, Ms., Sir, or Ma'am.
5. Require your child to use respectful words.
6. Require your child to use a respectful tone of voice.
7. Respect your child's God-given uniqueness and individuality by allowing her to make age-appropriate choices.
8. Make sure your child treats your home, furniture, toys, siblings' belongings, etc., with care.
9. Listen when your child speaks.
10. Be considerate of your child's needs.

4

HOW TO RAISE A BRAT

What would your parents have done if you looked them in the eye and said, "No"?

That's what I thought. Mine too.

My second-grade daughter and I were on a field trip. We had never been whale watching, and I was just about as excited as Ashton.

The note sent home to parents had just a few simple instructions: Dress warmly. No dairy products for breakfast (for you land lovers: milk = seasickness). Cameras may be brought by adults only.

Sounded easy enough.

We excitedly boarded the boat that would take us on our adventure out to sea. With every child fitted snugly into a life vest, our trip began.

A few moments into the voyage, one little girl asked her mother for their camera. Looking around to see if a teacher was watching, her mother cautiously handed her the expensive Nikon.

"Please be careful, Holly," her mother warned.

Holly leaned over the rail, ignoring her mother's plea.

"Holly, not so far over. You might drop the camera," her mother repeated.

Holly stretched up on tiptoes and poised herself over the edge, trying to catch a shot of a few nearby seals, acting as if she had not heard a word of her mother's warning.

"Holly, *please* be careful," her mother begged.

Holly stretched out over the edge a bit further.

"Holly, hand me the camera, right now, please."

With hands clamped tightly around the camera, seven-year-old Holly slowly turned to face her mother. Clearly, defiantly, she spoke.

"No."

Holly's mother looked a bit embarrassed but didn't say a word. Holly kept the camera until she was too bored to hold it any longer.

Holly had won.

No parent *wants* to raise a brat, but a quick peek into almost any mall, classroom, or park is all it takes to see that disrespectful kids abound. So who is parenting, or failing to parent, these kids? Surprisingly, I have found that often parents—even loving parents—unknowingly contribute to raising ill-mannered children by their parenting styles. See if you recognize yourself in any of the following parenting types.

The Repeating Parent

"Come away from the street, Ryan."

"Ryan, did you hear me? I said, 'Come away from the street.'"

"Ryan, if you come away from the street, you can play with the ball."

"Ryan. *Ryan.* Come here, Ryan."

Three-year-old Ryan never did come away from the street. And his father? Well, when Ryan ignored his wishes, he just shrugged and went back to pruning his rose bushes.

This scenario illustrates the Repeating Parent parenting style.[1] And although a repeating parent is easy to spot from a distance, it may be hard to see yourself as one. Do you ever find yourself saying the same thing over and over and over? Ever feel as though your child doesn't listen to a word you say? If so, you may be a repeating parent. Although being a repeating parent seems harmless enough, it can be fatal, for repeating parents unknowingly train their children to ignore what they say. How do they do it? By being "all bark and no bite," as the old expression goes. When a child knows words will not be followed up with action, the child learns to tune the parent out and do his own thing. Repeating parents subtly teach their children they don't have to be listened to, heeded, or held in high esteem. In short, and almost always unintentionally, repeating parents train their children to be disrespectful.

The Threatening Parent

A close kin to the repeating parent is the threatening parent.[2] Those who use this parenting style repeat their wishes over and over but add the element of threat. Phrases such as "If you don't . . . ," "I mean it," "I'm going to count to three," and "I'm not going to say this again" (but they do) fill their commands.

Although their tone of voice often becomes firmer, their actions don't follow suit. If repeating parents illustrate "all bark and no bite," threatening parents embody it. Their empty threats become personal reminders that they are not in charge. Rarely do these parents say what they mean and mean what they say. And their kids know it. The result? Disobedient, disrespectful kids and stressed out parents who feel like they live in a zoo.

The Doormat Parent

She gulped her juice down as quickly as her mother had poured it. Without looking up, she shoved her cup high in the air and demanded, "More juice." No "Please." No "May I?" Just "More juice."

What did her mother do? She hopped up, leaving her dinner, and scurried across the kitchen to quickly pour her little blond princess "more juice."

Was there a "Thank you, Mom"? Of course not.

This doormat parent was subtly training her child to disrespect her mother and to develop an unhealthy sense that the world revolves around her.

Doormat parents allow their children to speak rudely, make demands, and challenge authority. Doormat parents are often easygoing personality types, adults who have trouble asserting their own boundaries, or people who like to avoid conflict. In their effort to maintain peace at any cost, doormat parents frequently allow their children to treat them as peers or friends. Sometimes they even fear disciplining their children appropriately.

When a child learns that he can treat the most significant adult in his life—his parent—as a peer, he becomes arrogant, self-centered, and demanding. Children raised this way become abrasive and often have difficulty maintaining positive relationships, especially relationships with authority figures such as teachers, coaches, and later in life, bosses.

Doormat parents abdicate their God-given role of training their children to become healthy, unselfish adults. They don't *intend* to raise disrespectful kids, but they do.

The "Do as I Say, Not as I Do" Parent

"I don't get no respect."

Comedian Rodney Dangerfield created an entire persona around this plea. Some parents find themselves in the same quandary, and for many the reason can be traced back to their own behavior.

Parents who desire to raise respectful children but show disrespect to others around them—including their children—typify the "Do as I Say, Not as I Do" parenting style.

What do "do as I say, not as I do" parents look like? You may see them treating a server or cashier rudely. Or you may notice their disrespectful behavior with their own elderly parents or in-laws. Maybe you'll catch them breaking the drop-off procedures in the carpool line, showing a lack of respect for rules. Perhaps you will notice them demeaning their child verbally or physically.

The bottom line? Apart from modeling respectful behavior, it is impossible to raise a respectful child.

The "She's Lost Her Marbles" Parent

"You kids are driving me crazy," she yelled as she stomped down the hall, her pink terry cloth robe flying behind her like Superman's cape. Normally she was Supermom. But not this day. This day she was super mad.

We ducked for cover, my sister, brother, and I. And then we began to giggle. She was as angry as a bear before breakfast, but to us it seemed hysterical.

She's lost her marbles, we thought.

Is there a parent on the planet who hasn't been a "she's lost her marbles" parent at one time or another? I doubt it. Losing your cool from time to time comes with the territory of parenting. But losing your marbles as a habit or way of life is a real problem.

When a parent allows herself to be controlled by anger and yells or screams at her child, the child looks surprisingly, not at his own behavior, which is often the source of parental anger, but at the ridiculous behavior of the parent. It works like this: Johnny misbehaves. Instead of immediately dealing with the misbehavior, we repeat ourselves, threaten without consequences, or try to ignore the problem. When the behavior continues (as it usually does), we become so exasperated that we "lose our marbles," often yelling or screaming in anger. We "let our child really have it" in hopes of changing his behavior.

Unfortunately, little Johnny is so totally engrossed in either (a) how ridiculous we look and sound or (b) how he can steer clear of our anger, that he fails to see the importance of changing his behavior. The focus becomes *our* behavior, not his.

Not only is the "She's Lost Her Marbles" parenting style ineffective in changing undesirable behavior, but it subtly trains a child to disrespect his parent. After all, who would respect someone who consistently loses their marbles?

The Inconsistent Parent

Forrest Gump was right.

For some children life is like a box of chocolates—they never know what they're going to get. Such is the case for a child raised by an inconsistent parent.

Yes, kids will be kids. But kids who are not taught appropriate behavior will remain children even when they become adults.

Inconsistent parents change rules and boundaries depending on their mood, level of exhaustion, circumstances, or interest. One day this parent might be strict, demanding obedience at every point, while the next day she doesn't bother to follow through in any way.

Although no parent is consistent 100 percent of the time, the danger in an inconsistent parenting style lies in the message it sends to the child. When a child never knows where the boundaries are drawn or how Mom or Dad will react, she learns that the most significant people in her life can't be trusted. Quite simply, inconsistency equals insecurity for a child. And where there is an absence of trust, an absence of respect is sure to follow.

The "Kids Will Be Kids" Parent

They sat enjoying their lunch while their two children ran like miniature Michael Jordans around the restaurant. This was no Burger King, Taco Bell, or McDonald's. No, this was a normally quiet restaurant where families as well as business-people often dined. When the other diners began to comment on the children's rowdy behavior, they simply smiled as if to say, "Kids will be kids."

Yes, kids will be kids. But kids who are not taught appropriate behavior will remain children even when they become adults.

"Kids will be kids" parents often have easygoing personalities and are not easily upset. Or, if they were raised in an overly strict home, they may be attempting to avoid making the same mistake. In either case, these parents rarely correct their children. "She's in the terrible twos"; "He's a typical teenager"; "She's just tired"; "He's hungry" are their mantras. Although at times legitimate, when used repeatedly, these phrases mask an undercurrent of parental laziness, ignorance, or guilt.

Often the homes of "kids will be kids" parents are disorganized, with toys, books, and papers strewn everywhere. Although they don't go for the strict disciplinarian style of parenting, they still desire a relaxed, peaceful family life. But without respect, that is impossible to attain. Why? Because when children have no structure or boundaries, chaos reigns.

53

The Overly Strict Parent

Remember the line from the old western, "Shoot first, ask questions later"? This typifies the Overly Strict Parent parenting style. If you eavesdrop on an overly strict mom or dad, the most frequent word you will hear is "no." Rules go beyond the basic "no hitting," "no name calling" variety. Rules are many and enforced to the letter.

In their effort to control all, overly strict parents ultimately lose all control.

Overly strict parents make most, if not all, decisions for their children—even insignificant ones like what clothes to wear or what food to order at a restaurant. Children are not often asked, but told. The nurturing aspect of parenting is sometimes overlooked in overly strict homes. For overly strict parents, rules become more important than relationships.

Although overly strict parents want to raise respectful children, this parenting style often creates an atmosphere for rebellion to flourish. In an effort to attain independence and flee parental control, children of overly strict parents many times reject their parents' value system and sense of morals. In their effort to control all, overly strict parents ultimately lose all control.

The Overly Permissive Parent

The overly permissive parent stands in direct contrast to the overly strict parent. While one seeks to gain control, the other seeks to give it away. Statements such as "We never had any rules growing up," "I can come home whenever I feel like it," "Sure, I can see that R-rated movie," "I eat whatever I want when I want it," and "My mom (or dad) won't care" can be heard from children raised by overly permissive parents.

Often the message that overly permissive parents desire to send is "You are free to choose." The message that is most often heard, however, is "My parents don't care." In an effort to give their children freedom, overly permissive parents wind up rearing children imprisoned by insecurity and bound by the chains of self-doubt, fear, and lack of self-control.

The "It's Not My Child's Fault" Parent

"You'll never believe the conversation I just had," my teacher friend commented. "Every teacher at school knows all about Brandon [not his real name]," she continued. "He bullies. He's rude. He doesn't listen or complete assignments. I'm trying my best to reach out to this kid, to connect with him in some way, but it just isn't working. After talking with his mother, I know why: she won't face his problems. It's always 'another kid's fault,' or 'inadequate teaching,' or some other lame excuse. Until she comes to terms with her child's needs and inadequacies, the poor kid has no hope."

Imperfection doesn't mean your child will turn out to be a brat. But failing to deal with your child's imperfections does.

No parent wants to hear the dreaded words, "Can I speak with you about your child?" We all want our little darlings to be perfect. But they are not. And neither are we.

Imperfection doesn't mean your child will turn out to be a brat. But failing to deal with your child's imperfections does. Even the best kids have room to improve and grow. Making mistakes isn't fatal. Failing to learn from mistakes is. A child cannot learn from his mistakes if his parent is constantly defending him or blaming others for his poor choices.

Loving parents *do* believe the best about their children. They do protect. They do defend. But they don't ignore potential problems. They face them head-on with love, compassion, and wisdom.

"It's not my child's fault" parents firmly entrench their heads in the sand, staunchly defending or excusing their children's behavior no matter how blatantly impolite or inappropriate the action. Because a child raised by an "it's not my child's fault" parent rarely has a chance to acknowledge his mistakes, he doesn't have the opportunity to learn from them.

The Absent Parent

There are at least four million latchkey kids in the United States. According to *Child Trends'* latest research brief:

> In 1999, 15 percent of 6 to 12 year olds were in self care. ("Self care" means the children either took care of themselves or stayed alone with a sibling age 12 or younger on a regular basis, even for a small amount of time.) On average, children left unsupervised spent nearly 4-and-a-half hours per week alone or in the care of a young sibling.
>
> Children in low-income families, in general, are slightly *less likely* to be in self care than children in higher-income households, especially when they are young. In 1999, 12 percent of 6 to 12 year olds in low-income families were in self care versus 17 percent in other families.[3]

Millions of kids are virtually raising themselves. Is it any wonder that civility has all but disappeared in today's youth?

Even in homes where parents are not physically absent, many parents fall prey to the emotionally absent syndrome. Busy with household chores, charity work, hobbies, telephone conversations, the computer, or any number of other distractions, a physically present parent can be relationally absent. The outcome of either type of absentee parent is the same: children with little or no parental guidance who flounder socially, emotionally, academically, or spiritually.

No one wants to raise a brat. Not you. Not me. Not anyone we know. But the fact remains that ill-mannered kids are out there. We hear them in the grocery store. We teach them in Sunday school. We watch them on the soccer field. We might even live with them in our own home. So, who's raising these misguided children?

- Repeating parents
- Threatening parents
- Doormat parents
- "Do as I say, not as I do" parents
- "She's lost her marbles" parents
- Inconsistent parents
- "Kids will be kids" parents
- Overly strict parents
- Overly permissive parents
- "It's not my child's fault" parents
- Absent parents

You don't have to fall prey to these ineffective parenting styles. Armed with wisdom, courage, and God's grace, you can battle the temptation to employ these unproductive methods of child rearing.

You don't want to raise a brat. And you don't have to.

5

MANNERS MADE EASY

No Nagging Required

Nag. Nag. Nag.

It should have been a relaxing lunch. The food was delicious, the atmosphere quaint, and the outdoor weather perfect for a mid-afternoon meal at the newest cafe in town. Instead, I was distracted by the mother and preteenage daughter seated next to me.

"Sit up straight, Jessica. Put your napkin in your lap, Jessica. Don't chew with your mouth open, Jessica. Eat your vegetables, Jessica." Jessica silently rolled her eyes. Jessica's mother just sighed in exasperation.

The tension between mother and daughter mounted. Just observing their one-sided conversation was enough to stress *me* out.

No healthy parent wants to be a nag. We know it doesn't work. Yet too many parents fall prey to this ineffective method of teaching manners. Have you ever found yourself repeating the same old things over and over and over? Have you found yourself sounding like—horrors!—Jessica's mother? Probably.

Raising a mannerly child is no easy task—especially when you are having one of "those" days. You know the kind I mean. The kind of day on which your child . . .

- complains
- whines
- pitches a temper tantrum (or two, or three, or four)
- bites, pinches, or hits
- tells you "no"
- won't cooperate
- has a bad attitude
- makes every inconvenience a drama
- disobeys
- interrupts
- forgets responsibilities

Ever had a day like that?

It had been one of "those" days for me. As a relatively new, extremely exhausted, and very exasperated mother, I needed good advice in a big way. So I picked up the phone and called the expert—my mother.

"What should I do?" I pleaded.

I will never forget her advice: "Honey," she replied patiently, *"the trick to parenting is to stay one step ahead of your child."*

Proactive Parenting

To this day, I can't recall the specific childhood crisis that motivated my call, but the parenting principle I learned is still with me some seventeen years later. And whether your child is eighteen months or eighteen years, the principle is the same—the trick to parenting is to stay one step ahead of your child.

We stay one step ahead of our children by anticipating what's coming next in their lives. When we anticipate possible scenarios, we are better able to equip our children to behave in appropriate ways and to succeed.

Let's face it. Our homes are no fun if Jason can't sit still at the dinner table, Susie demands rather than asks, Jessica hasn't learned to share, and Michael grunts rather than speaks in complete sentences. Yet millions of us live in environments like this. There has to be a better way!

Many of us are caught in an unhealthy and ineffective web of relating to our children as "reactive" parents. If Jason can't sit still, we react. If Susie demands, we respond. If Jessica won't share, we smile in embarrassment and let her have what she wants anyway. When Michael speaks in monosyllabic grunts, we explain it away as typical teenage behavior. We react to our child's behavior *after the fact*. While it is often necessary to react to our child's behavior, effective parents also "proact." Proactive parents not only react to their child's behavior, they also proactively teach their child acceptable behavior *before* the fact.

> *The trick to parenting is to stay one step ahead of your child.*

Proactive parents are intentional about teaching their children right from wrong, acceptable versus unacceptable, and appropriate versus inappropriate behavior. Proactive parents equip their children to succeed in life by purposely teaching their children the values and behaviors necessary for success. They don't just hope their children will learn these things; they make sure they do.

Proactive parenting is the secret to raising well-mannered children. It makes teaching manners easy (or at least easier!) and learning manners fun. Proactive parents impart good manners without nagging, criticizing, or discouraging. Proactive parents stay one step ahead of their children.

Proactive parents teach and train their children in four key ways. Each is a progressive building block on which successful parenting stands. Proactive parents raise confident and courteous kids by (1) rehearsing, (2) reminding, (3) reinforcing, and (4) reflecting.

Want to raise a well-mannered child without ever nagging again? Become a proactive parent.

Rehearsing

"Thank you for dinner, Mrs. Porter. It was delicious. May I be excused, please?"

Every adult at the table stared open-mouthed in awe at four-year-old Ryan. I gazed in admiration at Ryan's mother.

No child learns manners by osmosis. Children must be taught. You can be sure that Ryan didn't spout out his gratitude for dinner on his own initiative. Without a doubt, Ryan's parents had rehearsed this moment, and when the moment came, Ryan knew what to do.

Proactive rehearsal is more than simply telling your child what to do. Plenty of parents tell their children what to do and still end up raising out-of-control kids. Proactive rehearsal involves showing your child what to do and allowing your child to practice.

The best way to begin is to choose just one skill you would like your child to learn or improve. Attempting to teach your child more than one skill at a time is certain to leave your child overwhelmed and you frustrated. Pique your child's interest in learning this skill or pick a skill your child is eager to learn already. Seize a teachable moment, such as an upcoming special event or sleepover or party your child plans to attend. Young children can be motivated by allowing them to learn a "big girl" or "big boy" thing. With older children you may want to appeal to their desire to be likeable or feel more self-confident. Show your child how learning this particular good manner will benefit her or how not learning it will hinder her.

Next, teach the skill in a relaxed, fun environment. It's OK to be silly and have fun teaching manners. Now is not the time to lay on the pressure or give a sixty-minute lecture. When I teach the Confidence & Courtesies class, I often do silly, exaggerated things, such as chew with my mouth open or talk too loudly or answer the phone with a "Yeah, what?" to show the children how "bad" manners look. We all end up laughing, and the kids get the picture of why good manners are important.

"What we learn with pleasure we never forget." —Alfred Mercier

Finally, rehearse with your child. It is not enough to tell your child what to do; you must practice with your child as well. Experts tell us that we remember only 20 percent of what we hear, 30 percent of what we see, and 50 percent of what we see and hear. Yet we remember a whopping 90 percent of what we see, hear, and *do*.

So lug out that old toy telephone or cell phone to practice phone manners; introduce your child to her father or brother or sister to practice meeting others; allow your child to set the dinner table to learn table manners. Knowing which plate is my salad plate and which is my bread plate, for instance, helps me behave with proper manners at the table. Practice and rehearse whatever you wish your child to learn. You'll stay one step ahead of your child, and your child will be prepared to succeed in becoming a person who loves and respects God and others.

Reminding

So, all we have to do is rehearse with our child and she will supernaturally become a miniature Emily Post, right?

Get real.

Yet, if we are honest, this is sometimes what we expect. We find ourselves becoming exasperated with our child when we must remind her of something we *know* she has been taught. I've seen it a hundred times—and I've done it myself. Most likely, so have you. It goes something like this:

"Lauren, did you thank Mrs. Smith for having you over to play today?"

(*Meekly*) "No . . ."

(*Exasperated*) "No? Why not? Lauren, you *know* better!"

And off we drive, either lecturing Lauren all the way home, or equally as bad, simply dropping the subject all together. Either way, we feel like parental losers.

A better way is to embrace the necessity of reminding our children about the kind of behavior we expect—kind, considerate, appropriate, behavior—*before* the fact, not merely after.

While children do need to learn personal responsibility, and as they grow older our reminders should become less frequent, we, as parents, need to realize that reminders are a vital part of a child's learning process. If we view reminding as part of raising our well-mannered child, it can free us from becoming frustrated moms and dads.

I don't know how many times I have reminded my children about good party manners while on the way to celebrate a friend's birthday.

"What will you say to Mrs. Barker when you leave?"

"Thank you for having me."

"Will you ask for the biggest piece of cake with the rose on top?"

"No!"

"What will you say when you are given food or a drink?"

"Thank you."

"What should you do if they play a game you don't like?"

"Play anyway, with a happy attitude."

Similar scenarios have been played out in my SUV with topics ranging from party manners to meeting adults, to being in a place of business, to sitting quietly at church, and most recently, job interview skills and dating etiquette. You name it—we've role-played it. And these conversations have served as necessary reminders to help my children live out a life of love and respect for others.

But refreshing our children's memories about appropriate behavior doesn't stop when the seat belts are unbuckled and car doors slammed shut. No, children, especially younger children, often need prompts to remember their manners. This especially holds true for toddlers and preschoolers. You can be sure that a three-year-old birthday girl will need to be reminded to thank each child for his or her gift as she rips into two dozen assorted toys, dress-ups, and games—all just for her. Count on it. Anticipate it. Rehearse it. And when the time comes, prompt it. Give your little birthday girl a moment or two, just in case she remembers on her own. But if she does not, gently ask, "What do you say?" If you have instructed and rehearsed beforehand, this is usually enough to prompt your child to politely say, "Thank you."

During my children's early years, I found this same gentle reminder useful to help them in a number of different situations. Upon meeting an adult, a sweetly whispered "What do you say?" reminded my daughter to look the adult in the eye and say, "It's nice to meet you." When leaving a friend's home, a gentle "What do you say?" reminded my son to say, "Thank you for having me." When my young children have inadvertently gotten up from the dinner table without being excused, "What do you say?" has reminded them to say, "Thank you for dinner, Mom. May I please be excused?" For older kids one-word prompts, such as *napkin, posture,* or *tone,* can be effective ways to remind your child about proper behavior. Through the use of repetition and prompts, children come to make these niceties habits of their own. They become not just your manners, but theirs. And moment by moment, day by day, you begin to tame your family zoo.

Note that the way in which we remind our children is every bit as important as the reminder itself. If our reminders are barked as commands or said in a way that embarrasses or demeans our children, we will most certainly not raise confident kids who love and respect God, themselves, or others. Gentleness is imperative. We are to encourage our children, not exasperate them. We can encourage them to become kind and considerate people when we use gentle reminders to help them learn.

Reinforcing

To proactively raise well-mannered children, parents must rehearse and remind. But these parenting tools are incomplete without reinforcement. Reinforcement is what causes us to repeat or delete a behavior. It is the feedback all human beings need to make a life skill a life habit. Reinforcement is the parental tool that will motivate your child to choose good manners not simply because you say so, but because he wants to.

So how do we effectively use reinforcement? First, it is important to note that reinforcement can be positive or negative. Positive reinforcement causes children to want to repeat a behavior. Negative reinforcement causes them to not want to repeat a behavior. Positive reinforcement rewards desirable behavior, while negative reinforcement penalizes undesirable behavior. And, at various times, both forms of reinforcement can be helpful.

Some of the most obvious forms of positive reinforcement include sticker charts, rewards, and, my favorite, praise. Make sure to compliment your child's polite behavior. Don't forget to pass along compliments you receive about your child. Encouragement reinforces your child's efforts to behave with good manners.

Positive reinforcement can also take subtler forms, like a look of approval or a feeling of well-being. Your child's polite behavior is reinforced by your smile and by her own sense of accomplishment. The benefits of utilizing positive reinforcement cannot be underestimated. Often, though, in their quest to be "superparents," moms and dads will set up elaborate charts and systems with which to reward their child for good behavior. While this works for some highly organized people, most parents end up overwhelmed with a system that looks like it was set up for NASA. Fortunately, it doesn't take elaborate schemes and flow charts to positively reinforce a child. Often it's the simple things that communicate best. Children would much rather see the light in your eyes and hear "well done" from your lips than receive toys or games that eventually wind up in the bottom of a toy chest or closet. Make it your practice to catch your kids being good, and you just might be surprised at how "good" they become.

Negative reinforcement can also be a powerful motivator when used wisely. But it's hard to allow your child to experience the pain of negative reinforcement. It's hard to follow through. Hard, but necessary.

It was 7:30 p.m. on a school night. A warm May evening had lured all the neighborhood children outdoors to play, including my then six-year-old daughter, Ashton.

"It's time to come in now, Ashton."

"Mom, can't I have just a few more minutes? I'm not quite finished playing with my friends."

"No, Ashton. It's dark outside!"

"But, Mom, you don't understand. I *love* people!"

Yes, our Ashton loves people. In fact, she loves people so much that she has invited herself over to friends' houses on numerous occasions. Even after I explained that inviting herself to someone else's home was impolite, Ashton's precious extroverted personality got the best of her. That is, until a little negative reinforcement was put into action.

Ashton was told clearly that, with my permission, she could invite friends to our home. She could not, under any circumstances, however, invite herself to others' homes. If she received an invitation for a playdate and I found out that she had initiated it, not only would she not be allowed to go, but she also would have to miss the next playdate on her busy social calendar. All was well until we received a phone call inviting Ashton to play. After a few questions on my part, it became obvious that this social rendezvous had been the brainchild of my youngest daughter.

It would have been so easy to allow her to go. It would have meant no tears, no broken heart, no disappointment. But it also would have meant no change. So, with a heavy heart, I declined the invitation, hung up the phone, and turned to face a child with tears as large as lemon drops streaming down her cheeks.

That was the last time Ashton invited herself to someone else's home.

To become a confident and courteous individual who loves God and others, a child must be allowed to experience the consequences of her behavior—both good and bad. To shield a child from the uncomfortable consequences of her undesirable actions is to stunt her emotional and social growth.

It has been said that people only change when they learn enough that they are able to, are motivated enough that they want to, or hurt enough that they have to. What is true for adults is true for children. Sometimes allowing our children to experience the uncomfortable consequences of poor choices is the best way to help them change undesirable behavior.

In the name of "protecting" their children, many parents naively guard their children from experiencing the consequences of poor choices. But doing so prevents their children from feeling the hurt that may be necessary for positive change. The result of this kind of parenting has been to raise a generation of children who fail to take personal responsibility, who act as though the world revolves solely around them, and who whine when inconvenienced and lash out in anger when things don't go their way. Children raised in this way turn into selfish, immature adults who struggle in their relationships, in their careers, and in life. In the meantime, their homes are usually chaotic and their parents often stressed. Life doesn't have to be this way. The solution lies in the power of reinforcement.

Reflecting

In addition to rehearsing, reminding, and reinforcing, it is important to reflect with our children about their behavior. To reflect means "to show an image of; to think seriously." In other words, reflecting occurs when we help our children think seriously about their behavior and the image it creates.

Reflecting is particularly crucial for older children and teens. One effective way to help children reflect on their behavior is to ask questions about their behavior. For instance, asking, "What do you think about how you answered the phone?" "What kind of impression do you think you made?" and "How do you think you could improve?" helps a child to think seriously about how her manners reflect an image of who she is. Asking questions opens the door for children to think about their behavior and the impression their manners, or lack of them, make on others.

Sometimes I find it helpful to reflect on the importance of good manners by discussing another child's behavior with my child. Asking a child questions such as "Did you notice Ryan's attitude at the party? What did you think about it?" is a great way to enlighten a child about why good manners are important. Becoming aware of another child's manners—whether good or bad—provides an important visual image for your child. Children, like adults, often have blind spots when it comes to their own behavior, so by observing the behavior of others, they can become enlightened about their own behavior. To avoid gossip and comparisons, observing the behavior of children they do not know is best.

Not long ago my daughter Kylie and I were doing some back-to-school shopping in one of the trendiest stores for pre-teen fashions. We overheard an exchange that went something like this:

"Ashley, honey, here's a cute shirt. What do you think of this?"

"Mom (*said with a roll of the eyes*), no way. I hate it!"

Her mother was silent.

(*A few minutes later*) "Ashley, I found some pants you might like."

"Mom, you pick out the dumbest things. Just don't even try."

About thirty minutes later, Kylie and I rounded up our purchases and headed off to the cash register, where we stood in line right behind—guess who?—Ashley and her mother. Kylie and I exchanged glances as we overheard the whopping total Ashley's mother spent on her—four hundred dollars! Ashley ungratefully snatched up her bags of clothes, and without so much as a "Thanks, Mom," marched off a good ten steps in front of her mother.

Seizing this event as a teachable moment to reflect on the value of polite, respectful behavior, I turned to Kylie and asked casually, "What do you think about how Ashley treated her mother?"

Boy, did Ashley's conduct give us a lot to talk about! Kylie and I discussed everything from the importance of respect for one's parents to the magnitude of the tone of voice we use, to the significance of being a grateful and gracious person. I left the store knowing I had made more than an investment in my daughter's outward beauty; more importantly, I had made an investment in her inward beauty.

And all it took was a few moments of reflecting on behavior.

Rehearsing, reminding, reinforcing, and reflecting—these are powerful tools in the hands of a proactive parent. With these tools parents can effectively raise confident, courteous kids without nagging, criticizing, or discouraging. Remembering that the key to parenting is to stay one step ahead of your child, which of these building blocks do you need to put into action beginning today?

Beginning today, how will you . . .

Rehearse with your child?

Remind your child?

Reinforce with your child?

Reflect with your child?

6

IT'S ALL ABOUT ME—OR IS IT?

Greyson was really no different than any other thirteen-year-old. Like most teenagers, Greyson lived his life as if the world revolved around him. And like most parents, Deborah and Greg scratched their heads wondering, *What happened to our sweet, darling boy?* Self-centered one day and thoughtful the next, most teenagers are a study in contrasts. But Greyson's ego-driven behavior began to drive his family crazy.

Discouraged but undaunted by Greyson's attitude, Deborah and Greg planned a family mission trip to an orphanage for AIDS babies. Preparations for the trip were disheartening, to say the least. Greyson complained at every turn. "Do we *have* to do this? This will be such a drag," he moaned. Greyson's attitude left Deborah and Greg wondering if maybe they could leave Greyson at the orphanage for a few weeks.

Greg, Deborah, and their two children arrived at the orphanage intending to stay only an hour or two that first day. Five minutes after their arrival, a tiny child approached Greyson. "Daddy, hold me," the little dark-haired boy said to Greyson, arms outstretched in anticipation. To Deborah and Greg's surprise, Greyson scooped up the child and held him tightly. Other kids surrounded Greyson and his younger sister, Julia, eager to play with kids a little older than themselves. Greyson carefully set down the outgoing child he held in his arms and hesitantly began to play with the other children. He was particularly drawn to one tiny newcomer to the orphanage. Found living alone, eating nothing but dog food, this wide-eyed four-year-old captured Greyson's teenage heart.

For what seemed like mere moments, Greyson and Julia wrestled and romped with the orphaned children whose bodies were poisoned with the deadly virus. One hour turned into two. Two hours turned into four. From morning until night they played with their newfound friends.

At last Greyson and Julia consented to leave. Later that evening Deborah emerged from the shower to find Greyson sitting at the foot of her bed.

"What's up, buddy?" she asked.

"Mom, this was the best day of my whole life," Greyson began, his face beaming. "I want you to know that the boy you saw today, the boy that played with those kids—that was the *real* Greyson. I'm sorry I've been so selfish lately."

Does parenting get any better than this?

"That's not fair!" "You owe me." "I want." Ever hear these words in your home? Odds are you have. Children come into this world believing that life revolves around them. One of parents' greatest responsibilities is to cultivate an "others-centered" attitude in their children. The ability to view others' needs and feelings as important is foundational to becoming a person who lives by the Golden Rule. Jesus also taught that "it is more blessed to give than to receive" (Acts 20:35). But in today's me-centered, consumer-oriented culture, this idea is believed by few and practiced by even fewer. The result? Adults and children who live selfish, empty lives. But parents can and must teach their children to break free of the "it's all about me" attitude.

It Starts with Me

Paradoxically, learning to be others-centered starts with you and me. It begins with our attitude, behavior, values, and choices.

How I live my life and how I treat those around me will inevitably rub off on my children. If I hoard my things, think only of myself or my immediate family, or spoil my kids, the possibility of raising a selfless child will be next to nil. When I treat others with kindness, share my possessions with those less fortunate, volunteer my time, and give freely of myself to others, the odds of raising a thoughtful, unselfish human being greatly increases. Raising a child who lives not as a self-centered ego-maniac, but rather as a contributing, productive member of society, is directly dependent on how I live my life.

Because the pull of the human heart to be selfish rather than selfless is so strong, parents must seek opportunities to impart the value of unselfish living.

Values are caught, not merely taught.

But because the pull of the human heart to be selfish rather than selfless is so strong, parents must seek opportunities to impart the value of unselfish living. Basics like sharing, taking turns, or allowing another to go first all contribute to raising an unselfish child.

Your child must experience firsthand the promise of Jesus that "it is more blessed to give than to receive." Thirteen-year-old Greyson experienced it. Four-year-old Chantel experienced it too.

Each morning, Chantel's dad, Michael, read Chantel a Bible story at breakfast. Chantel seemed particularly interested in the story of the good Samaritan they read one bright fall day. Careful to put concepts into words her preschool mind could grasp, Michael explained how the good Samaritan showed love to a person in need. After the story was read and their cereal eaten, Michael closed his Bible, kissed his strawberry blond, pigtailed daughter good-bye, and watched her bound out their door for a morning at preschool.

At noon, Chantel's mom, Michelle, promptly picked her up from school and headed for a local fast-food restaurant. Mother and daughter had developed a special ritual on Tuesday and Thursday afternoons that included a lunchtime treat for Chantel. Down the familiar road they traveled, but on this day they witnessed an unfamiliar sight. There, by the road, stood a man with a sign, "Homeless. Please help."

"Mommy, why is that man standing there?" Chantel asked.

"Because he is homeless," answered Michelle.

"What does his sign say?"

"It says he needs help," Michelle replied.

"Can we help him?" Chantel asked innocently.

"Well, Chantel, today I only have four dollars in my wallet. I was planning on taking you to lunch as a special treat. We don't have money to buy your lunch and the homeless man lunch too."

Chantel paused.

"Mom, I want to buy the man lunch. Can I, please?"

A few minutes later Chantel proudly shoved four wadded dollar bills across the counter of the closest fast-food restaurant to purchase lunch for the homeless stranger. Back in the car, Michelle slowed so Chantel could hand her new friend his meal. "God bless you," she called, her face beaming like sunshine.

Michelle smiled contentedly at her daughter's compassion for one in need, but not a word was spoken about the incident—that is, until Chantel heard the sound of her father's key in the front door later that evening.

"Daddy, Daddy," Chantel cried, running to Michael as fast as her little legs could carry her. "Today I was a good *American.*"

Chantel was a good American—and a good Samaritan. But her heart and her eyes were prepared by parents who taught her the value of unselfish living. Raising a child who thinks not only of herself extends much further than teaching her to perform a few perfunctory courtesies. It is a matter of her heart.

Teaching a child to see the needs of others need not depend solely on events like feeding the homeless or caring for AIDS babies. Learning to be unselfish can, and should, be imparted during the everyday events of life.

Developing empathy—the ability to identify with another's emotions—or sympathy—compassion for another's situation—takes a child out of his own world and into the world of those around him. Opportunities for developing empathy and sympathy are as near as our own backyards.

Children can learn that they shouldn't hit, bite, call names, or participate in other hurtful behaviors by picturing how they would feel if they were hit, bitten, or called names. Ask your child questions such as, "How do you think you would feel if Tommy hit you? Would you like it? Would it make you feel mad?" "What if Jennifer called you a hurtful name? How would you handle it?" "Remember when Jason wouldn't share with you? How did you feel?" When you help your child see the world through the lens of another, you help your child develop empathy. A child who can put himself in another's shoes will be an emotionally healthy adult who can live an others-centered, rather than a self-centered, life.

Experts tell us that the foundation that enables a child to develop empathy is laid during infancy. When a baby cries and her needs are met, she learns to trust; she comes to understand the connection between expressing a need and having the need fulfilled. As her needs are met, a child begins the critical process of attachment. The ability to attach is the cornerstone for the ability to empathize. As a parent, then, the importance of responding to our child's needs cannot be overstated. In other words, we help develop a compassionate child when we treat our child with compassion.

Although children can be notoriously self-centered, they can also show signs of deep and sincere compassion. Watch for moments of compassion on your child's part. When your child helps his brother or sister, take note and praise your child for his kindness. When your child shows compassion to a hurt friend, comment on his thoughtfulness. Reinforce the positive behavior you see in your child, and your child will soon learn the value of human kindness and unselfish living.

Values are caught, not merely taught.

Another way you can aid your child's unselfish emotional development is to provide the means for your child to serve others. Yesterday my daughter Kylie and I volunteered at our church's food pantry. What an exhilarating feeling we both had knowing we were doing something to help people! Some families, ours included, have adopted a child through World Vision, Compassion International, or some other relief organization. Another family I know passes out church bulletins together during Sunday morning church services. Still others volunteer to help with vacation Bible school. Some families visit nursing homes, read to young children at local libraries, or make meals or cards for shut-ins. The opportunities to serve others are endless. But in all likelihood, your child will not choose to serve others unaided by you. The pull of video and computer games, playing with friends, and just hanging out is strong. For your child to learn to serve, not just be served, the tide must turn, and you, as the parent, must turn it!

Pick an achievable service project for you and your child. Choose one that stirs your heartstrings, or better yet, let your child choose a project that stirs his. Start small. Don't make serving complicated or difficult. Let your child experience firsthand the joy of unselfish living.

Children gain a sense of self-worth not merely by being told how worthy they are, but by behaving in worthy ways. When children demonstrate unselfishness, work hard to accomplish a goal, or see a project through to completion, they develop a sense of self-respect or worth. When we rob our children of opportunities to work hard, give to others, or make personal sacrifices, we also rob them of the tools they need to become emotionally healthy individuals who can take care of themselves and others.

Children, like adults, need to be needed.

Ten-year-old Heather's mother enrolled her in a "technical performance" class held at their local church. Designed to teach children the ins and outs of sound, lighting, and other technical aspects necessary for performance, Heather had no idea that she would develop a knack for such things. Nor could she have predicted how much she would come to enjoy it. So when the director of Sunday school asked for volunteers to help run the sound system on Sunday mornings, Heather eagerly offered to help.

Sunday after Sunday Heather faithfully arrived to serve her fellow classmates by running the sound board. At first her participation was enthusiastic. But when weeks turned into months, Heather's interest began to wane. One Sunday, feeling a bit under the weather, Heather decided to take a day off from her duties. Since she had never missed a Sunday and she was feeling a bit sluggish, her parents decided to allow Heather to stay home.

When Heather returned to her duties the next week, she inquired about the previous Sunday.

"Heather, it was terrible. We didn't have any sound. We sure did miss you!" her Sunday school teacher innocently remarked.

Later Heather's mom confided in the Sunday school director. "Wow! I've never seen Heather so committed to anything. Once she realized how needed she is, nothing could make her miss her Sunday morning service."

I would venture to guess that Heather's participation and service to others gives her a feeling of satisfaction like no other. Heather's wise parents allowed her to serve. They encouraged her to serve. And both Heather and those she serves reap the benefit. It *is* more blessed to give than to receive.

But many parents, in their efforts to make their children happy, unknowingly rob their children of the ultimate source of happiness—living a selfless life. Selfish people are unhappy people. When we contribute to our children's selfish tendencies by refusing to allow them to serve, saying things like, "You're too busy to volunteer for that," or "Let me do it for you," we unwittingly contribute to their ultimate unhappiness. Selfish people do not know how to love. Therefore selfish people cannot know or enjoy the pleasure of relationships. Their friendships and family relationships will suffer. And, as an adult, their marriages and parenting will suffer.

We surely don't want this for our children.

Resist the Temptation to Spoil

Have you, like me, noticed the "I'm entitled" mentality prevalent in many of today's youth? Where does the notion of entitlement come from? Quite simply, it comes from being (as my wise grandmother used to say) "spoiled rotten." And just whose fault is it if my child is spoiled? Mine.

Our children will never break out of the "it's all about me" perspective as long as we allow life to be all about them. When we give in to the whims of our children, bribe our children to behave with the promise of the latest toys and gadgets, or overindulge our children, we contribute to an "I'm entitled" mentality.

Twelve-year-old Natasha's (not her real name) mother had labored for weeks to give her the perfect birthday party. Wanting to do something extra-special for Natasha, she planned a train ride for Natasha and several of her friends from their hometown to the big city about an hour away. Once there, the girls were treated to dinner at Natasha's favorite restaurant and a movie of Natasha's choice. All seemed to go smoothly until the moment came for Natasha to open her gifts. Natasha's mother had collected the presents and put them in a bag for safekeeping as the girls boarded the train, hoping to relieve the giddy preteens of the burden of caring for the packages.

But when the moment came for Natasha to open her gifts, her mother realized her mistake. The presents were missing! Frantic, she placed a call to the train station hoping that some kind soul had found the bag laden with Natasha's birthday gifts and had turned them in. No such luck. The train station contacted the train conductor, and still no presents were to be found. Natasha's mother mentally retraced her every step and called each place she and the girls had been. Sadly, her efforts proved unsuccessful.

Natasha's mother was heartbroken and laden with guilt. How could she have done such a thing? Where could the presents be? Literally feeling sick to her stomach, she broke the bad news to Natasha.

"I'm so sorry, Natasha, I must have left your presents on the train. But, honey, I will try to replace them the best I can."

"What?" Natasha demanded. "How could you lose all my presents? You *will* replace them. Every one."

Natasha remained angry with her mother for weeks. Even after her mother tried her best to replace the missing gifts, Natasha still was not satisfied.

"This sweatshirt is black. The one Molly bought for me was blue," Natasha complained. "Jennifer's gift was a Hurley shirt. You bought me a Roxy shirt. I don't want it if it's not the same. Take it back."

Natasha's mother hung her head in shame.

Natasha's true story, though extreme, occurs in lesser ways in homes throughout the country. In every neighborhood, on every block, a spoiled child can be found. These kids set the rules and rule the roost. Leaving their parents feeling impotent, these kids have been led to believe that life revolves around them. They personify the "it's all about me" mentality.

What do these children really need? They don't need more stuff—that's for sure. They need structure, boundaries, and discipline. They need parents who follow through rather than make idle threats. And they need love. Real love—the kind of love that helps a child break out of the chains of self-centered living and into the freedom of unselfishness.

If you want to raise an unselfish child, a child who has learned that it is more blessed to give than to receive, then resist the urge to spoil your child.

Summing It All Up

Jesus gave us the Golden Rule. "Do to others as you would have them do to you," he said. "It is more blessed to give than to receive," he taught. We raise children to follow these principles by living out these values ourselves, by providing opportunities for service, and by resisting the temptation to spoil our children. Children raised this way will certainly be blessed, and no doubt, so will those around them!

Tips to Help Your Child Break Out of the "It's All about Me" Mentality

1. Model unselfish living by being kind to neighbors, store clerks, servers, people in line behind you at the grocery store, etc.
2. Plan a service project for you and your child.

3. Teach your child to allow guests to go first, choose what to play, have the larger portion of food, etc.

4. Resist the temptation to spoil. Say no every once in a while and stick to it.

5. Teach your child the importance of gratitude. Have your child write a thank you note to someone who has recently given her a gift or shown her special thoughtfulness.

6. Talk to your child about the importance of helping others.

7. Teach your child to hold the door open for others.

8. Surprise yourself and your child! Help someone when you least expect to.

9. Teach your child to say, "Excuse me," when he bumps into someone.

10. If your child wants to serve, give to, or help another person, let her do it if at all possible.

PART 2

TRAINING YOUR CHILD

Let the Training Begin!

Congratulations! You have laid the foundation for raising a well-mannered child by completing the first half of this book on training yourself to be a trainer. Now you are ready to begin the practical, real-life task of training your child.

This section has been divided into six separate sections—one main manners concept for each of six weeks. While it is fine to read ahead, it is best to implement one skill at a time. Trying to cram too many etiquette rules into your child's brain and behavior will leave both you and your child frustrated. Instead, work on one skill a week. After seven days, or when the skill has been (somewhat) mastered, move on to the next skill. Manners are building blocks that must be reinforced and repeated over time, but the basics can be taught in just a few weeks.

Week one's lesson, "Everyday Manners," is quite comprehensive for the simple reason that many manners should be used every day. These "everyday manners" are numerous and broad, but don't let the scope of these manners overwhelm you. Simply pick one or two you feel would most benefit your child at this time.

Scientists tell us that learning occurs gradually and in steps. Animal trainers routinely teach behaviors in small bits. We would do well to follow their example. As the old saying goes, "Things are hard by the yard but a cinch by the inch"!

Are you ready to tame your family zoo? Let the training begin!

7

WEEK 1

Everyday Manners
for Everyday Monkeys

Don't you just love a polite kid?

You know the one I mean: the kid who says, "Thank you," without being reminded; the kid who asks by including "please"; the kid who shares; the kid who speaks when spoken to; the kid who knows when to talk and when to listen; the kid we want our child to marry; the kid we want our child to be.

Every day opportunities abound to be kind or rude, thoughtful or thoughtless. These moments occur at home and at school, in the playroom and in the classroom, on the field and off the field, in public and in private. Every moment of every day parents and children can treat others with kindness and consideration. Or not.

Like all behavior, using good manners is a matter of choice. Using proper etiquette is making a choice to show kind and considerate behavior. Good manners are behaviors based on respect and care for others. "Everyday manners" should be used so often that they are part of the way your child relates to others as a way of life. And since everyday manners begin in the home, they should be a part of the way you relate to others as well. Your personal example will lay the foundation for every teachable moment.

Please and Thank You

Nearly every child over the age of two—most likely including your child—knows "the magic word." But does your child use it? Perhaps no other words go further to promote civility, respect, and an attitude of gratitude than the words *please* and *thank you*.

My brother-in-law, Christian children's music artist Dean-o (of Dean-o and the Dynamos) wrote a song a few years ago entitled "Rad-Dude Attitude"[1] to help kids think and behave like God wants them to think and behave.

Rad-Dude Attitude
(From Philippians 2:5–11)

You gotta have a
RAD-DUDE attitude
It's a RAD-DUDE attitude
It's a can do too attitude
It's an attitude of gratitude
A RAD-DUDE attitude!

Cleary, this "rad-dude attitude" is an attitude of gratitude. Who doesn't want to raise a grateful child—a child with a "rad-dude attitude"? But how do you do it?

You can begin to teach this basic skill in your child's earliest years. Just as you enthusiastically coax your child to say, "Dada," "Mama," and "Bye-bye," you can also model "please" and "thank you." As soon as a child is old enough to point to communicate her wants, you may begin sweetly saying, "Please." As you hand her an object, say, "Thank you." When a child learns to say "please" and "thank you" from her earliest years, these words become part of her permanent vocabulary.

As your child grows, require "please" before getting her what she wants. When she asks for more juice without saying "please," simply remind her to say "please" before fulfilling her request. Help her remember to say "thank you" afterward.

Equally important as making a request with "please" is answering a question with "Yes, please," or "No, thank you." Don't allow your child to answer with "Nah," "Yuck," or "Nope." If you allow these responses at home, your child will certainly use them at others' homes.

Along with teaching "please" and "thank you," teach your child to say, "You're welcome" and "Excuse me." "Excuse me" should be used when leaving the table or bumping into someone and after sneezing, coughing, or making other bodily noises.

The words *I'm sorry* may be the most difficult words to master in any language, but they are vital for the existence of peace and harmony. Teach your child the value of these words by saying them yourself when you handle things in less than perfect ways.

When your young child needs to apologize, help her find the words she needs by saying something like, "Tell Molly you're sorry you broke her toy." If your child resists, don't engage in a power struggle, but do apologize by saying something like, "Molly, I'm sorry Megan broke your toy. Let's see if we can fix it." Give attention to the offended child, not the resistant child. You don't want to reward impolite behavior by giving a rude child attention.

Finally, use "please" and "thank you," "Excuse me," "You're welcome," and "I'm sorry" as part of your everyday vocabulary. Remember the old saying "The apple doesn't fall far from the tree"? Perhaps this is seen most vividly in the way kids speak. Kids become like their parents, so be the kind of person you wish your child to become. Families who speak to one another using these words have less stress, conflict, and tension, because kindness pervades the atmosphere.

Behavior with Adults

Perhaps no manners have become as lax in our generation as children's manners with adults. We already discussed the importance of teaching your child to respect adults in chapter 5, but teaching your child specific behaviors will help him communicate his respect for adults.

- Adults should be addressed as Mr., Mrs., Miss, Ms., Dr., Reverend, etc., unless they give your child permission to do otherwise. It is also appropriate for your child to address adults as "Sir" or "Ma'am."
- When introduced to an adult, a child stands, looks the adult in the eye, shakes his or her hand, and says, "It's nice to meet you." Very small children need only to say, "Hi" or "Hello."
- At formal dinners children stand by their chairs until all adults are seated. Children wait until an adult begins eating before they begin.
- Children allow adults to go first unless otherwise directed.
- In conversation children answer questions adults ask with more than "yes" or "no." If an adult asks, "Do you like school?" help your child be ready to say something like, "Yes, especially reading and art."

- Children should acknowledge people they know with a "Hi, Mrs. Connors" or "Hello, Mr. Green." This includes neighbors, adults who drive carpool, teachers they pass in the hall at school, parents of friends, and any other adults they know. Sometimes children find this embarrassing, but to ignore an adult makes a child seem unfriendly or rude.

- When waiting at restaurants, on a crowded bus or subway, or in other public venues, children should offer their seats to adults.

- Children do not interrupt adult conversations except in case of emergency. If a child must interrupt, she should say, "Excuse me, Mom."

- Children listen to adults and do as they say without complaint (barring, of course, anything inappropriate, illegal, or immoral).

- Children help adults—especially the elderly, women with babies, or pregnant women—by opening their doors, carrying heavy packages, or helping in any way needed.

Behavior in Public

Kids running in stores, nearly knocking others down; kids wiggling and giggling during church; kids talking during class time or during a movie—we have all witnessed these events, maybe by our own children.

Why? Because children are children. They do not naturally think about the consequences of their behavior on others. It's our job to teach them. Public manners become a way for your child to develop an unselfish lifestyle.

The following behaviors may be for children, but adults can benefit from following these rules as well. Teaching your child to abide by these "dos and don'ts" is a surefire way to ensure that your child behaves politely in public.

In Public

Don't . . .

- use loud voices
- run indoors
- talk in movies, at church, during class, or in other public places where others are trying to listen
- cut in line
- stand or sit too close to others
- use others' personal belongings without permission
- treat a store like a playground
- stand in shopping carts
- talk when others are speaking
- comb your hair, bite your nails, or pick your nose or your ears

Do . . .

- take turns
- wait your turn
- say "excuse me" if you bump someone or are bumped
- hold doors open for others
- apologize with a sincere "I'm sorry" for anyone you inconvenience
- say a warm "thank you" to anyone who offers to help you; this includes carpool moms, bus drivers, librarians, teachers, and coaches among others
- stay beside parents unless given permission to do otherwise
- cover your mouth when you cough, sneeze, burp, or yawn
- stay seated and still when traveling on a bus, train, or plane; bring a book, quiet toy, and/or snack to keep occupied

- place your trash in trash cans rather than throwing it out of a car window or leaving it on the ground or on fast-food tables
- chew gum quietly; do not blow bubbles in public. Wrap chewed gum in a tissue and place in a trash can rather than throwing it on the ground.

Behavior with Strangers

Teaching your child how to behave with strangers can be tricky. On one hand, you must warn your child about the dangers of speaking to strangers. On the other hand, you want your child to be friendly and polite when meeting someone new. What's a parent to do? Sit down with your child today and make sure she knows the following seven rules for dealing with strangers.

1. *Do not* speak to a strange adult when alone or when no other adult is present, even if the stranger knows your name.
2. *Do not* answer a stranger's questions. A sincere adult in need will ask another adult for help, not a child.
3. *Do not* go near a stranger's car.
4. *Do not* accept anything from a stranger, including candy, gum, or toys.
5. *Do not* answer the door by yourself unless given permission by a parent or caregiver. Do not open a door for strangers.
6. *Do not* leave a house, yard, or playground without permission.
7. *Do not* give out personal information when chatting on the Internet.

As a parent, teach your child the value of introductions. When your child is introduced to a stranger by a friend or relative, your child may respond politely and warmly. While you want to guard your child from harm, do teach him to apply the manners for public places with all people.

Handling Personal and Public Property

A Sunday school teacher was discussing the Ten Commandments with her five- and six-year-olds. After explaining the commandment to "honor your father and your mother," she asked, "Is there a commandment that teaches us how to treat our brothers and sisters?" Without missing a beat, one little boy answered, "Thou shall not kill."[2]

Nothing can cause more frustration, and even anger, between friends and family members than dealing with a person who does not handle another's personal property with care. If you have more than one child, you have probably witnessed this frustration firsthand. The child who breaks another's toy, uses siblings' personal items without asking, or enters a sibling's bedroom or bathroom without knocking is sure to cause conflict.

Frustration between siblings over "unauthorized use of personal property" happens with siblings in every home—mine included. Take a look at the "Terms of Property Use" my son, Taylor, created for his sisters when he was in seventh grade.

Terms of Property Use
Under the authority of Mr. and Mrs. John Paul Jones, it has become necessary for Taylor Jones, middle school student and U.S. citizen, to create a new policy concerning the personal possessions and properties of Taylor Jones. The new policy will endeavor to keep all personal items of any sort strictly under the ownership of Taylor Jones. Kylie and Ashton Jones are under no circumstances (with exception of emergency, as defined as an immediate physical danger) allowed to obtain and/or utilize the possessions of Taylor Jones without first seeking permission by Taylor Jones. In the event that Taylor Jones should be absent

or distracted beyond conversation, Mr. or Mrs. John Paul Jones will either confirm or deny permission to use one or several of Taylor Jones's possessions.

The following are additional terms and/or regulations that are included in this policy. Prior to entering the room of Taylor Jones, one must knock and wait to obtain permission to enter. In the event that Taylor Jones is placed in a position in which he is granted authority over Kylie and Ashton Jones (babysitting), full and absolute respect and obedience are required. When allowed use of one of Taylor Jones's Play Station games, Kylie and Ashton Jones are obliged to place it back in its proper case upon completion of use. If given permission to obtain and/or utilize, an unquestionable respect of that item is absolutely necessary.

If Kylie and Ashton Jones agree to comply with this new policy, Taylor Jones will be obliged to decrease the amount and degree of verbal harassment as well as comply with any of Kylie and Ashton Jones's terms. However, upon repeated abuse of this policy without a reasonable excuse, a fifty-cent toll will be charged for the use of Taylor Jones's property.

Conflict between siblings over use and abuse of personal property may be annoying, but more serious is the growing mass of kids who think nothing of abusing public property. In their minds, defacing and destruction are mere games rather than serious and costly actions punishable by law. Children must be taught the value of personal and public property—and the earlier they are taught, the better. Here are some things you can do to ensure that your child understands the importance of handling others' things with care.

- Require siblings to ask before using a brother or sister's personal item.
- Require older kids and teens to knock before entering a sibling's room.
- Talk to your child about respecting personal and public property. For instance, when you and your child see graffiti, discuss how it got there, the consequences of

95

graffiti for our environment, the cost of cleaning it up, why defacing property is against the law, etc.

- Make sure your child follows simple rules such as "Keep off the grass" and "No dogs allowed," and make sure you follow these rules too. When you reinforce posted signs, your child gets the signal that public property is to be respected. When you break these rules, you send a message that rules are for everyone else, not you or your child.

- Have your child replace, repair, or pay for any item she damages. Even a small child can learn the value of property by doing small chores to earn money to contribute to replacing a broken or damaged item.

- Have your child clean up his own messes. Noted home organization expert Emily Barnes says her family motto is "Don't put it down. Put it away." This motto will serve you and your child well, whether at home or away.

- Don't litter or allow your child to litter.

- Give your child the responsibility of household chores. These should include the care of his own room—making the bed, picking up toys—and additional chores depending on your child's age. Caring for pets, taking out trash, unloading and loading the dishwasher, setting the table, and folding clothes are chores that can be delegated to school-age children. As your child grows, you may want to include taking care of the lawn, doing laundry, cleaning the bathroom, etc.

- Chores should not be considered optional, nor should you pay your child for her weekly chores, although you may pay your child for any additional work she does over and above her normal responsibilities. These tasks teach your child responsibility, the value of contributing to the family, vital life skills, and the importance of caring for personal property. Even if you can afford outside help, give your child her share of household responsibilities, for without them your child cannot fully appreciate the value of things.

Basic Hygiene

A conscientious mom told her four-year-old son that he had to have a bath.

"Why do I have to take a bath?" he whined.

"Well, honey, you've had a big day," she replied.

He thought about this for a moment and then asked, "So, if I have a little day, I don't need a bath?"

Kids don't usually associate personal hygiene with good manners, but in fact, the two go hand in hand. It's not very pleasant to stand next to a person with body odor or speak to a person with bad breath. Teaching your child personal hygiene is an essential ingredient of everyday manners.

Preschool-age children can learn the importance of brushing their teeth, taking a daily bath or shower, and washing their hands before dinner and after using the restroom. It is often older children, however, that need constant reminders to do these things. Until puberty sets in and your child becomes interested in the opposite sex, reminding him to take care of basic grooming will probably be part of life.

Many parents find reminder charts helpful to keep from having to constantly ask, "Did you brush your teeth?" Try placing a list with morning and evening "to dos" on your child's bathroom mirror if your child needs constant reminding to take care of his personal hygiene.

Every day your child should:

- take a bath or shower, including cleaning ears with a washcloth
- wash her hands before eating

- brush his teeth morning and evening. Teeth should be brushed *after* bedtime snacks. Teach your child to floss regularly.
- comb or brush her hair
- wear deodorant if needed. The need for deodorant usually begins in about the fifth grade, although this varies depending on the child's rate of physical maturation.
- wash hair at least every two to three days. Kids involved in active sports will probably need to wash their hair every day.
- Keep fingernails and toenails trimmed. Kids play hard, and dirt inevitably finds its way under even the cleanest child's nails. Keep fingernails on the short side to avoid the "dirt under the fingernail" syndrome. Fingernails and toenails should be trimmed in private and the clippings placed in the trash.
- Teens need to shave regularly. Show your child how to properly shave and make sure he or she has the proper tools (new razors, shaving cream) to make this milestone easier.

Everyday Manners for Everyday Monkeys

The manners your child learns today will lay the groundwork for his interactions with others throughout his life. What kind of person will your child become? It depends in large part on his "everyday" manners. From the playroom to the ballroom, from the classroom to the boardroom, everyday manners will help today's child succeed tomorrow.

Beginning today, pick one, two, or three everyday manners you plan to help your child master this week. Remember that "things are hard by the yard but a cinch by the inch." Soon you'll be on your way to taming your family zoo.

Training Schedule

Training Tips

1. Play the "What If?" game. Use these suggestions as a springboard for your own questions.
   What would you do if . . .
   - a stranger asked you for help?
   - you bumped into someone?
   - a friend's parent brought you home?
   - your sister borrowed your shirt without asking?
2. Make a grooming chart that includes both morning and evening rituals. Place it on your child's bathroom mirror.
3. Have your child open doors for you. Thank him or her.
4. Talk with your child about expected behavior *before* an outing or event this week.
5. Have your child address adults as Mr., Mrs., Miss, or Ms. if she doesn't do so already.

Manner I plan to teach:

How I plan to train:

Tools I will need:

Reinforcement I will use:

8

Week 2

Meeting and Greeting
Requires More than a Grunt

I liked her immediately. Her sweet smile and confident demeanor drew me to her like a bee to honey.

Her stylish blue and red dress hung elegantly on her perfect frame. Her black hair, cut in a pageboy, glistened like silk. When she spoke everyone seemed to take note, and I knew I wanted to be her friend.

You remember her too. She was in your school and in mine. She was the queen of first grade. My recollections of meeting her are as clear today as they were more than thirty years ago.

How long do you think it takes to make a first impression? One minute? Two minutes? Experts tell us that a first impression is made within ten seconds of meeting someone new. Based on nothing more than the external images of clothing, hairstyle, size, shape, and demeanor, we size one another up.

"Do I like her?" "Is he friendly?" "What kind of person is she?" "Should I trust him?" Innately, almost unconsciously, we judge others within the first ten seconds. And whether for better or worse, first impressions are often lasting impressions.

Fortunately, making a good first impression can be as simple as following the rules of introductions. Yes, meeting and greeting others requires more than a grunt, but it doesn't have to be difficult and it can be fun!

When a Child Is Introduced to an Adult

When a child is introduced to an adult, the use of six simple gestures is all it takes to make a good first impression. Teach your child the acronym "SHAKES":

S—Stand Up

A child should always stand when introduced to an adult unless he his physically unable to do so (squeezed into a row of stadium seats or balancing food on his lap, for instance). Standing up when introduced to an adult shows respect for that adult.

H—Handshake

Children should shake hands when introduced to an adult. The importance of a good handshake can't be overestimated and is easy to learn.

- Begin with fingers together and thumbs pointed up.
- Engage hands "web to web."
- Never offer only your fingertips.

Handshakes should:

- last about three seconds
- be firm but should not hurt
- take only two or three pumps

A—Answer Questions Asked

Interested adults often ask children questions about themselves. Your child might be asked questions such as "How old are you?" or "What grade are you in?" Prepare your child to answer any question she is asked by speaking clearly (kids are tempted to mumble when meeting adults!) and looking the adult in the eye.

K—Keep Focused

Children are easily distracted by any number of things. But when meeting an adult, a child should politely stay still and focus on the person he is introduced to.

E—Eye Contact

For many children, eye contact is the most difficult part of learning to be introduced. Let's face it: meeting someone several feet taller and many years older can be intimidating. But eye contact is essential when introductions are made because it communicates interest and respect.

S—Smile and Say, "It's Nice to Meet You."

How pleasant it is to meet someone who smiles and says, "It's nice to meet you"! Right away these people exude warmth and confidence. Your child should also say, "It was nice to meet you," at the end of a conversation with a newly introduced adult or peer.

103

There is no better way to teach your child the SHAKES basics than to practice, practice, practice. When you know your child will be in a situation in which he is likely to meet new people, especially adults, talk with him beforehand about how he should respond. Make sure he knows how impressive his good manners will be and how much fun it can be to meet new people. Role-play with your child in a fun, relaxed way until he feels confident about meeting others.

When the big moment arrives for your child to meet an adult, his practice will likely provide him with the tools and confidence he needs to respond politely. If your child freezes, you may gently remind him to say, "It's nice to meet you," but refrain from embarrassing your child by excusing his behavior with comments such as, "He's shy" or "He always does this." Don't force your child to hug or kiss someone he is meeting for the first time—even a relative. Introductions can be awkward and intimidating for children, so allow the basics of SHAKES to suffice.

Learning to Make Introductions

Every child knows it is no fun to be left out. When your child introduces friends who haven't yet met, she helps everyone feel included and helps ensure that no one feels excluded. An introduction should be made anytime your child is with two or more people who do not know each other.

Talk with your child about the importance of making introductions, then practice using the following rules.

The Three Rules for Making Introductions

1. *A boy is always introduced to a girl.* Therefore, you say the *girl's name first.* "Brittany, this is Josh McDaniel."

2. *A younger person is always introduced to an older person.* Therefore, you say the *older person's name first.* "Mr. Green, I would like you to meet my brother, Jason."

3. *A person under authority is introduced to a person with authority.* Therefore, you say the *person with authority's name first.* "Reverend Michaels, may I introduce Miss Gray?"

Your child should also know that when making introductions, a person's position is considered first, then age, and finally gender. So, if your child introduces an elderly man and a young woman, the man's name should be said first. Also, I find it easier to remember that if a person has a title (President, Reverend, Mayor, etc.) that person's name goes first, no matter what his or her gender or age.

To make learning these three rules of introductions fun and easy, try providing your child name tags with fictional or famous names written on them. Take turns making introductions as people like "President Bush," "Judge Judy," "Michael Jordan," or "Sponge Bob." You'll both have fun and learn in the process.

Of course, your child should know that if he can't remember these three rules of introductions, he should make an introduction anyway. Better to make an introduction with the "wrong" person's name first than to fail to introduce at all.

Use this chart below to help you and your child learn the three rules of introductions.

First Name in Introduction	Introductory Phrases	Second Name in Introduction
Girl	This is	Boy
Older person	I'd like you to meet	Younger person
Person with authority	May I present	Person under authority

105

How to Introduce

The following are guidelines for making an introduction.

- Speak slowly and clearly.
- Look at each person while saying his or her name.
- Use phrases such as "This is," "I would like you to meet," or more formally, "May I present?"
- Use first and last names. *"Pam, I'd like you to meet Ryan Adams. Ryan, I'd like you to meet Pam Andrews."*
- Say something about each person. *"Mom, this is Kevin Smith. He's on my soccer team. Kevin, this is my mother, Mrs. Jones."*
- When introducing one person to a group of ten or fewer, introduce the newcomer informally to the entire group. *"Hey, everybody, this is my friend Sarah Miles."* Then introduce the new person to each member of the group individually.
- In a larger group of ten or more, introduce a newcomer to the host and the first two or three people nearby.
- If your child is the newcomer and no one offers to introduce him, he should introduce himself to an unoccupied individual or friendly looking group by saying something like, "Hi, I'm Jared Smith, Molly's neighbor. What's your name?"
- If your child forgets a person's name (and we all do!), she should simply apologize and say, "I'm sorry, I have forgotten your name." Teach your child to repeat a new person's name to help her remember it the next time. The more we use a name, the more likely we will remember it.

Going On from Grunts

Once an introduction has been made, relationships can develop. Your child's relationship with others will depend in large part on her conversation skills.

A conversation is much like a game. Just as you take turns when playing catch, kickball, or cards, a good conversationalist knows how to take turns in a conversation. All kids know that it is no fun to play with a ball hog. When someone dominates a conversation, it is like tossing a ball that the other person doesn't throw back. Eventually the other players get bored and leave the game. In the same way, kids who talk too much soon find themselves without friends because they have failed to "toss the ball" in conversation.

Help your child master the art of communication by teaching him the following guidelines.

How to Listen

I graduated from UCLA with a degree in interpersonal communication. While I was there, a study was conducted to determine what qualities make others perceive someone as a good conversationalist. In other words, researchers tried to pinpoint what factors make us *like* to talk to one person and dislike to talk to another.

Can you guess the number one quality of a good communicator—the factor that most attracts us to *want* to talk to another?

Listening.

Yep. That's right. The most important quality of a good conversationalist has nothing to do with what he says but has everything to do with what he does. And what we want people to do for us is *listen*.

Your child should be aware that others will *want* to engage him in conversation if he is a good listener. Others will know your child is listening by his nonverbal communication. Communication is 90 percent nonverbal and only 10 percent verbal. That means the nonverbal cues, such as eye contact, nodding one's head in agreement with something said, and leaning toward the speaker rather than away, all communicate that your child is listening.

Help your child learn these nonverbal skills by modeling them. When your child speaks, *listen*.

Sometimes this is easier said than done.

Real Life

It had been a busier than usual day for the thirtysomething mom and her four kids. Work, errands, household responsibilities, and carpooling the older kids to after-school activities filled every minute. Her youngest child, a precocious four-year-old, tended to talk nonstop. Frankly, most of what this youngster said went in one ear and out the other as she hurried from one activity to the next. It was 6:20 p.m. before she stood in front of her kitchen sink trying her best to prepare a quick but healthy dinner for her hungry brood.

If you have a nonstop talker who wants your attention every waking moment, instead of responding with "In a minute," try "For a minute."

On and on her little chatterbox continued to talk. The exhausted mom gave him the occasional "Uh-huh" and "Oh, really?" but she wasn't listening, and he knew it. Distracted by dinner preparations, she hardly noticed as her four-year-old dragged the step stool out of the kitchen pantry. Carefully he opened the step stool and placed it strategically next to his mother. He gently took his mother's face into his tiny hands and turned her face toward his own.

108

"Mommy," he whispered, with his chubby hands still tenderly holding her face, "you need a new set of ears."

How many times have my children had this unspoken thought? How many times have yours?

To teach our children to be good listeners, we must be good listeners ourselves. This doesn't mean that we can never have a little peace and quiet or that we need to put all duties on hold for our children's every whim. But it does mean that we need to make our children our priority—and that means listening.

If you have a nonstop talker who wants your attention every waking moment, instead of responding with "In a minute," try "*For* a minute." This way you give your child the attention he needs and can still accomplish the tasks you need to complete.

If, on the other hand, your child rarely opens up, seize the occasional moments your child does want to talk. For this child, "in a minute" or "for a minute" means "never." Your motto for parenting this child should be "Stop, look, and listen." When a quiet child begins to share, *stop* what you are doing. *Look* at your child. And *listen* to what he says and how he feels. Moments for sharing come infrequently for this type of child. If you fail to stop, look, and listen, these moments will be missed forever.

To teach your child to be a good listener, you must listen to your child—and go one step further. You must require your child to listen to you and to others. Do not allow your child to interrupt. Make sure your child looks at you when you speak to him. These are not only polite, respectful behaviors; they are the habits of the socially adept child.

How to Ask Questions

Suppose a new girl joins your shy son's class. Picture a cute boy sitting down next to your self-conscious teenage daughter. Imagine your middle-schooler being driven home by the family she just babysat for. Does your child know what to say? Does he or she sit in awkward silence, completely tongue-tied, or can your child carry on polite conversation?

If your child has ever been faced with the embarrassing dilemma of "What should I say?" (and who hasn't been?), the solution lies in learning to ask good questions.

Most people love to talk about themselves. Self-centered? Maybe. But true, nonetheless.

Asking questions is a surefire way to get to know another person. Questions open the door of discovery about another person—their interests, likes, dislikes, hobbies, values, and concerns. Asking questions will allow your child to uncover common areas of interests with others. By asking others questions about themselves, your child communicates concern for others.

Some questions lend themselves better to conversation than others. Closed-ended questions can be answered with "yes" or "no." "Do you like your math teacher?" "Are you in fourth grade?" "Do you have any pets?" are all examples of closed-ended questions. Though fine to start a conversation, these questions don't allow an individual to elaborate. The result? The conversation dies and awkward silence follows.

Open-ended questions, on the other hand, require more than "yes" or "no" answers. "What's your favorite subject?" "What do you think about your math teacher?" "What position do you play on the team?" all demand answers that actually *tell* you something significant about the individual answering the question. Open-ended questions get a conversation going and keep a conversation rolling.

How to Follow the Rules

The "game" of communication is played by a set of rules. As we have already seen, one of these rules involves taking turns.

But this is only the beginning. Good conversationalists have mastered the rules of communication. For most kids, these rules are learned unconsciously over the course of relating to friends and family. But if you have ever observed a socially awkward child, you no doubt noticed her inability to grasp socially acceptable rules of behavior. For some children these rules do not come naturally. Fortunately, these rules can be taught.

The Game Rules

- Maintain eye contact. Socially skilled kids look both peers and adults in the eye when conversing, but they do not stare. Eye contact should last only five to seven seconds.
- Maintain appropriate space. In American culture it is polite to stand about two to three feet away from someone during a conversation. However, this distance varies among cultures. In many Latin cultures, for instance, the distance is smaller and people feel comfortable standing closer.
- Be still. Kids can and should be active. But a kid who never winds down will overwhelm others with his constant activity. When your child speaks to others, teach him to stand still and stay focused.
- Use a polite tone of voice. This means no bossy or whiny tones. Children (and adults, for that matter!) should speak neither too softly nor too loudly.
- Be interested in others. Don't only talk about yourself. Ask open-ended questions that encourage others to talk about themselves.
- Smile. Kids with warm, friendly smiles inevitably have friends.
- When asked, "How are you?" your child should respond by saying, "Fine, thank you. How are you?"

- When others talk, listen. Help your child "see" how to listen by role-playing listening using only nonverbal communication.

Yes, meeting and greeting others requires more than a grunt. But mastering the art of conversation will enable your child to develop healthy, happy relationships that will enrich her life both now and throughout her lifetime.

Training Schedule

Training Tips

1. After explaining how to introduce and how to be introduced, provide your child with name tags of famous or fictional characters. Take turns introducing one another as "Sponge Bob," "Scooby Doo," etc.
2. Practice open-ended questions at dinner.
3. Use the one-word prompt *tone* to remind a child not to whine or be bossy or rude.
4. Practice "stop, look, and listen" with your child.

Manner I plan to teach:

How I plan to train:

Tools I will need:

Reinforcement I will use:

WEEK 3

Table Manners:
It's Feeding Time at the Zoo

Picture yourself seated at an elegant restaurant, ready to feast on all your favorite dishes. Perhaps the lights are low and warm candlelight glows softly. Maybe you're outdoors feeling the warmth of the sun and a gentle breeze relaxing all tension from your stressed-out muscles. Perhaps the smell of freshly baked bread and homemade desserts wafts from the kitchen.

Picture your child seated next to you.

Now how do you feel? Are you ready to enjoy a dream dinner or are you bracing yourself to endure a nightmare?

Table manners are the biggest challenge any parent faces when it comes to taming a family zoo. As every parent knows, kids aren't born caring about using silverware correctly or about disgusting fellow diners with half-chewed food or about staining clothing instead of using a napkin. But parents *do* care. And therein lies the challenge—and the potential for major family conflict.

Creating the Desire

You, no doubt, have the desire for well-mannered children. You want to be able to dine in peace. You long to take your child to any eating establishment, no matter how casual or elegant, and enjoy the experience. Almost certainly, your little monkey couldn't care less.

For a child, eating is strictly a utilitarian event. From his vantage point, as long as food gets in his mouth and his hunger is quelled, his dining experience has been a success.

What's the point in having to sit still? he wonders. *Who cares how I hold my fork? What's the big deal about chewing with your mouth closed? Why can't I eat with my fingers?*

Sometimes a picture is worth a thousand words.

They had no idea it was prom night when they decided to take their three daughters out to dinner. As it turned out, it was to be a more memorable evening than they had expected.

Was it the sight of the beautiful girls dressed in their elegant gowns, makeup and hair coiffed to perfection, that mesmerized my three nieces? Perhaps it was the sound of the laughter that pervaded the restaurant. Was it the boys, so dashing in their tuxedoes?

No, none of these things kept my nieces' eyes riveted to the large group of teenagers seated next to them. What caught their attention were the table manners of two of the girls in the party of ten.

All dressed up in her finery, one of the five girls sat down, legs spread apart, and proceeded to slurp her spaghetti slouched over her plate as if she hadn't eaten a meal for days. The drop-dead-gorgeous teenage girl seated two chairs away sat with perfect posture, napkin in her lap, eating her meal as if she had been trained by royalty. It was beauty and the beast in real life.

Now, my sister had been in the reminding stage regarding her daughters' table manners much too long, in her opinion. Like many of us, she had repeated, rehearsed, and reminded her girls until she was blue in the face. But nothing could have seared the importance of good table manners in their preteenage brains quite as profoundly as the real-life visual image they received that night.

You may not have the good fortune to witness a scene as eye-opening as my three young nieces, but you *can* create the desire for good manners in your child. Try asking your child about any kids in her class who chew with their mouths open at lunchtime. Do the other kids like to sit across from that child? Probably not. More likely, that child finds himself the brunt of cruel jokes. Your child doesn't want to be that kid.

More positive teachable moments include an upcoming wedding, formal event, or special dinner your child plans to attend. Before the big event, seize the teachable moment to instruct, model, and practice good table manners. Or create a teachable moment yourself. Plan and prepare a special dinner at home or treat your child to a special dinner—her choice of restaurants (which, by the way, may mean Burger King!) when she has mastered good table manners.

Kids aren't born caring about table manners. It's our job to teach them. Can a "happy meal" be more than a menu item at McDonald's? Yes—if you approach teaching table manners with a little creativity, ingenuity, and motivation.

To Teach Your Child to Eat, Eat with Your Child

Whether your child is two or twelve, one aspect of table manners must remain consistent for your child to grasp proper dining skills—your own good manners.

Modeling good table manners is the visible image your child needs to learn how things are done. If you chew with your mouth closed, place your napkin on your lap, and keep your elbows off the table, your child's transition from dining disaster to exceptional eater will be easier.

But in today's fast-paced society, this is often easier said than done.

Let's admit it. We live in a culture in which our afternoons and evenings are filled with soccer practice, dance lessons, and music instruction, and our streets are lined with McDonald's, Taco Bell, and Burger King. And so our children, who are so accustomed to dinner on the go, become woefully inadequate in practicing the etiquette skills necessary for success in social life. Is it any wonder that acquiring the finer points of table manners has escaped many of us?

Because of our on-the-go schedules, the necessity of teaching our children table etiquette becomes even more important. Although good table manners can and should be practiced when eating meals on the run, there is no substitute for eating a meal, however simple, together as a family. Besides allowing you to model and teach table etiquette, eating together will benefit your family in other ways.

Volumes have been written about how to keep teenagers out of trouble, but according to a study presented at the American Psychological Association's 105th Annual Convention, the best solution may be as simple as eating meals together as a family more often.[1] A 1994 survey of two thousand high school seniors by Lou Harris and Associates found that students who regularly ate dinner with their families four or more times a week scored better in a battery of academic tests than those who ate family dinners three or fewer times a week.[2]

Even teenagers see the value in family dinners. When asked by *Parade Magazine* to describe dinnertime, one teen gave this typical response: "Some families have a nice family dinner, like spaghetti and meatballs and apple pie or something else yummy that the mom cooks in her free time. But both my parents have to work. Some of my friends' moms will make dinner, and the dads will come home, and the whole family will sit and talk and have one of those really good meals. I wish we were like that. Then my busy family would have some time to talk to each other" (Danielle Lee, age thirteen).[3]

The evidence speaks for itself. Make family meals a priority. Turn off the TV, handheld games, phones, and laptops, and turn your attention to those you love. Don't focus on an elaborate meal if that's not your thing; instead, focus on your family.

To get conversation rolling, ask your kids specific things about their day. We like to ask, "What was your favorite thing you did today?" and "What was your least favorite?" Some families call this sharing their "highs and lows." Another fun game my husband made up during long car rides has become a conversation staple at our dinner table as well. He asks, "Would you rather . . . ," and then fills in the blanks with sometimes crazy, sometimes serious choices. For instance, "Would you rather be an Olympic athlete or a famous movie star?" "Would you rather be able to live underwater or fly?" Fill in the blanks with your own ideas and see how much you learn about your children.

Setting the Table

One of the best ways for a child to learn table manners is to learn to properly set a table. Sadly, even many adults lack this basic skill. In public nothing can spoil your dinner faster than feeling uncomfortable about not being sure which fork to use, which side your bread plate is on, or which glass is yours. In the working world, clients have been lost and job interviews have gone sour over avoidable faux pas at the dinner table. The solution to helping your child avoid these mistakes at any age is as simple as teaching him to set a table properly at home.

117

Basic Place Setting

Learning to set a basic place setting—the kind used at family dinners or casual meals—is the easiest and best way to begin teaching your child table manners. The basic place setting consists of a plate, glass, knife, spoon, fork, and napkin.

The knife and spoon are placed on the right side, while the fork is placed on the left. To help your child remember, remind her that the words *knife* and *spoon* each have five letters, as does the word *right*. *Fork* has four letters, just like the word *left*. The knife is placed on the inside next to the plate, blade facing in. This makes it easier to pick up the knife to cut food, but I like to tell my students that it also prevents anyone whose arms may be mistakenly on the table from getting cut.

Finally, the glass is placed on the right side above the knife and spoon, since most people are right-handed. The word *glass* also contains five letters, like the word *right*. The napkin is placed on the left either beside or under the fork.

Informal Place Setting

Once a child has mastered a basic place setting, it is time to master an informal one. Kids find setting a table this way fun because it is out of the ordinary for them. Even children as young as first and second grade are able to learn to set an informal place setting correctly.

As with the basic place setting, the dinner plate is placed in the middle with forks and napkin on the left; knives, spoons, goblets, and glasses on the right. Except for the dinner plate, all plates are located to the left of the diner. The salad plate (which is slightly larger than the bread plate, since a larger plate is necessary for salad than for bread) is placed to the left of the forks. The bread and butter plate is placed above the forks, with the butter knife atop the plate, blade facing down.

The water goblet and wine glasses are placed on the right above the knives, with the water goblet slightly behind the wine glass or glasses. I tell my students to remember to place the larger water goblet behind the smaller wine glass so the wine glass doesn't get lost and can still be seen.

Perhaps the single most important rule to remember when dining formally is to start with the outside silverware and work in. This rule of thumb is also useful in setting an informal table. In the United States, the first course is either an appetizer/fish

119

course or salad course. If no appetizer course is to be served, the salad fork is placed on the far left. The dinner fork is placed next to the salad fork. Finally, a dessert fork may be placed on the left next to the plate, although more commonly it is placed above the plate, with the handle pointing left and the tines pointing right.

A soup course usually begins the use of spoons, so the soup spoon is placed on the far right of the dinner plate. Next, closer to the plate, is the dinner spoon. The dessert spoon is placed above the plate, with the handle facing right and the "bowl" of the spoon facing left toward the forks. Knives are placed next to the plate, always blade facing in.

Napkins at informal dinners are usually found under or to the left of the forks, but they may also be decoratively folded in the center of the dinner plate or even in a goblet.[4]

Try letting your child have a go at setting the table this way for fun and watch her manners rise to the occasion!

Table Manners 101

At the age of three or four, your child is ready to learn the beginnings of proper table etiquette. You want your child to embrace good table manners as a life habit, not something reserved only for company. So, if possible, start early. Otherwise you may need to break some bad habits in order to replace them with good ones.

Basic table manners can be divided into manners used before dinner, during dinner, and after dinner. Try teaching—and modeling—the following rules of etiquette to simplify the mystery of dining.

Before Dinner

- Men and boys let girls walk ahead into the dining room. A girl stands behind her chair until the hostess sits down.

A boy or man should then pull out the girl's chair. Boys and men may then sit.

- Your child should wait until grace is said before placing his napkin in his lap. If grace is not to be said, your child should place his napkin in his lap after being seated. Teach your child to unfold his napkin into a rectangle shape as he places it on his lap (not tuck it into his shirt). At a formal dinner, your child should wait for the hostess to put her napkin on her lap first. At formal restaurants, the maître d' will place the napkin in your child's lap for him.
- Posture is important. When seated your child should sit up straight but be comfortable. She should place her hands in her lap when she is not using them. Elbows or forearms do not belong on the table while eating, but your child may rest her elbows on the table if no food is present.

During Dinner

- Your child should wait until everyone has been served before eating. If your child is dining in a very large group such as a banquet, he needs only to wait for those around him to be served before he may begin to eat.
- When eating, your child should bring her food up to her mouth, not her mouth down to her food.
- Your child should chew quietly with mouth closed. Instruct your child to swallow before talking.
- At a casual, family-style dinner, foods should be passed, not slid. Your child may reach for anything on the table that doesn't require him to stretch across either the table or his neighbor. When something is out of reach, teach your child to say, "Please pass the butter," not "I need the butter" or "I want the potatoes."

121

- Pass foods to the right. Serving dishes are passed counter-clockwise so that each person may help himself without the bother of two dishes reaching one person at the same time.

- If your child is asked to pass only the salt or the pepper, show her how to pass *both* the salt and pepper shakers together by holding them in one hand.

- To pass pitchers, gravy boats, or other serving pieces with handles, your child should pass them with the handle facing the person who requested them.

- At a restaurant, if your child is asked to pass the sugar, he should pass the entire sugar container, not one or two sugar packets.

- Your child should cut only one piece of meat at a time.

- To butter bread or vegetables, your child should cut butter pats, place the butter pats on her butter plate, pass the butter dish along to other diners, and then butter her food. Your child should not cut butter from the butter dish and place it directly on bread or vegetables. If no bread plate is provided, your child may place butter on her dinner plate.

- Your child should butter only one small piece of bread at a time unless she is buttering warm toast. If your child butters an entire dinner roll, she will likely get butter on the sides of her mouth when she attempts to eat it.

- When serving himself, your child should use the serving fork or spoon that comes with the serving dish. He should not use his own fork or spoon, which may spread germs.

- When using a napkin, your child should blot her mouth, not scrub it. If your child must leave the table during dinner, she should place her napkin on the seat of her chair. After dinner she may place her napkin to the left of her plate without wadding or crumpling it.

- Do not allow talk about unpleasant topics during mealtime. Bodily functions and gory stories are "no-nos."
- Your child should not play with or brush her hair at the table.
- Your child should not play with salt and pepper, sugar packets, creamers, or food items on the table.
- If your child invites friends to your home for a meal or even a snack, your child should serve guests first. Guests should wait for the hostess to begin eating before they begin.
- At someone's home, it is considered polite to take at least one serving of the main course that is served, even if your child dislikes it. Your child may refuse a fruit, vegetable, or dessert with a polite "No, thank you." Your child should *never* tell the hostess that he doesn't like the food she offers. If your child is allergic to certain foods, he should inform the hostess beforehand if possible.
- Your child should not place used silverware on the table. Instead, she should place the knife and fork side-by-side at the top of her plate. This is called the "rest position." Your child should rest a used soup spoon on the saucer underneath the soup bowl.

After Dinner

- When your child is finished with his meal, he should place his silverware in the center of his plate, fork tines up. This is called the "finished position."

- Before leaving the table, your child should ask her parent or host to be excused. She should thank the cook (even if it's her mom!) for her meal.

Table Troubles

No matter how refined one's manners, the occasional table trouble happens to us all. Who hasn't spilled a drink, dropped food, or had trouble cutting tough meat? If it can—and does—happen to adults, it will most certainly happen to children. The following tips will help you and your child navigate table troubles.

Taking Something Out of the Mouth

If your child bites into spoiled food or a bone, he should roll it back onto his spoon or fork with his tongue and quietly place it on his plate.

Spills

At home or at a friend's home, your child should quickly tell parents or host, apologize, and offer to help clean it up. At a restaurant she should tell the server and allow the restaurant personnel to clean up the spill.

Dropped Silverware

If your child drops silverware at someone's home, pick it up, set it aside, and ask for a replacement. At a restaurant, dropped silverware should be left on the floor. Your child may ask the server for a replacement.

Sneezing, Coughing

If your child needs to cough or sneeze, he should turn his head away and cover his mouth with his napkin. Your child should never blow his nose into a napkin. Your child should excuse himself to blow his nose into a tissue or handkerchief. Should blowing his nose in public become an absolute necessity, he should try to make as little noise as possible. Your child should not be allowed to burp or make other bodily noises at the table.

Food That Won't Stay on a Fork or Spoon

Your child may push food onto a fork with a piece of bread or a knife. She should never use her fingers.

Restaurant Manners

When a child learns proper table manners at home, using proper manners in a restaurant comes easier. As a parent, you can make this transition smooth and the experience pleasant for your child, other diners, and yourself by following a few guidelines.

125

- Be prepared. Have crackers ready in case the wait for your food is longer than expected. Stash paper and crayons in your purse or diaper bag to keep your child quietly occupied.
- Make expectations clear to your child beforehand. Explain the importance of remaining seated throughout the meal, talking quietly, and using good table manners.
- Be prepared to follow through with consequences. If your child is small and becomes disruptive, leave your table until your child is ready to rejoin the meal.
- Discuss menu choices with your child before your server arrives to take your order. Allow your child to order (if old enough) with "I would like the hamburger (chicken fingers, spaghetti), please."

Common Restaurant Terms

- *A la carte*—A menu with each item priced individually.
- *A la mode*—Served with ice cream.
- *Au jus*—Served in its own juice or gravy.
- *Amandine*—Served with thinly sliced almonds, sautéed in butter.
- *Du jour*—Of the day.
- *En brochette*—Cooked on a skewer.
- *Flambé*—Sauced with spirits and flamed before serving.
- *Florentine*—With spinach.
- *Gratin*—Topped with cheese and browned under a broiler.
- *Table d'hôte*—Fixed-price menu.
- *Vinaigrette*—An oil and vinegar dressing.[5]

Although learning table manners takes time and practice, the tools you provide by ensuring your child learns good table etiquette will prepare her for a lifetime of success.

Training Schedule

Training Tips

1. Allow your child to set the dinner table. If your child is young, start with an informal place setting. If your child is older, let him set a formal table with fine china, a centerpiece of his own choosing—the works!
2. Get your kids in on the action of preparing to have guests for dinner. Allow them to make place cards for children (or for adults, if you're brave), set a "kids" table, or prepare a simple dish.
3. Using an 11 x 13 inch piece of construction paper, have your child draw an informal place setting. Laminate the drawing (any copy shop can do this for a nominal fee) and let your child use it as a placemat.
4. Pick one manner you want your child to master. Discuss this manner with your child apart from mealtime. At the table use one-word prompts like *napkin, posture,* and *elbow* to remind your child to practice good manners.
5. Treat your child to a special dinner once she has mastered a specific table manner.
6. Allow your child to order his own meals when dining out.

Manner I plan to teach:

How I plan to train:

Tools I will need:

Reinforcement I will use:

10

WEEK 4

The (Telephone) Call of the Wild

The phone rings. Your little one scampers quickly toward the telephone shouting, "I'll get it!"

Most kids love to answer the phone, but few know how to answer it properly. The result? All too often callers are left trying to coax two-year-old Matthew into getting his mother, covering their ears as little Jamie screams, "Mom, it's for you!" or wondering if preteenage Ryan actually wrote down the message they left.

In this chapter parents will learn ways to foster good telephone etiquette in their children. But as every parent knows, our children's communication skills don't end when their ears aren't glued to the telephone receiver. Emails, instant messages, and cell phones are all a part of our kids' interactions with others. The next few pages outline proper manners for these forms of communication and more.

Tackling the Telephone

"Hello. This is the McLeod residence," said the confident little voice on the other end of the line.

"Hello, Brooke. This is Mrs. Jones. May I please speak with your mother?"

"One moment, please," Brooke responded without hesitation.

I could hardly believe my ears. Brooke was only four years old.

Whether a child is four or fourteen, the way she answers the phone determines the impression—good or bad—she makes on others. If your child answers the phone with a polite, "Hello, this is the ____ residence," she immediately puts the caller at ease. If your child answers with a mumbled grunt or is too young to say anything beyond "Hello," the caller is left wondering what kind of conversation will follow.

Just as important, the manners your child learns at home today are the manners she will take into life tomorrow. Every day we adults interact with others over the phone, transacting business, making appointments, or encouraging friends. The success or failure of these interactions depends, at least in some measure, on the social skills we have acquired. Your child's success, both now and later, is influenced by her social skills too.

Whether used for business or pleasure, the telephone is a great place to "connect." Teach your child the following basics to ensure her phone manners connect positively with others.

Answering a Call

- Your child should answer with a friendly "Hello," or "Hello. This is the Jones residence." Remind your child that the person on the other end of the line can't see him, so he should speak slowly and clearly without mumbling. Teach your child to put a smile on his face when answering a call. A smile on the face can be heard in the voice!

130

- If the caller doesn't identify himself, your child may say, "May I ask who is calling, please?" Your child should not say, "Who is this?" or ask who is calling immediately after saying, "Hello."
- If the call is for your child, he should say, "This is Josh," rather than "Speaking," "Yeah," or "It's me."
- If the call is not for your child, she should say, "One moment, please." You will be pleasantly surprised at how many callers will comment on your child's good manners when she uses this phrase.
- Your child should not yell for the person the phone call is for. He should lay the phone down gently and get the person instead. Nothing is worse than having a child scream, "Mooooom! Telephone!" into a caller's ear. A note of caution to parents: it is difficult to break this habit if *you* yell for others to come to the phone.
- If the person can't come to the phone immediately, your child should say something like, "Jason will be with you in a moment."
- If your child receives a phone call while she has a guest, she should keep the call brief or ask to return the call. It is impolite to have a lengthy phone conversation and ignore a guest.
- Teach your child to take phone messages. To help, make sure you keep a pad of paper and a pen or pencil next to the phone. Your child should repeat the caller's name

> ## The Right Way to Make and Receive a Telephone Call
>
> *"Hello. This is the Smith residence."*
>
> *"Hello. This is Garrett Johnson. May I speak with Joey, please?"*
>
> *"One moment, please."*

and phone number to make sure he has written it down correctly.

- If your child receives a wrong number, she should simply say, "I'm sorry, you have the wrong number."
- If your child is home alone, instruct him to never tell a caller that his parents are out. He should say something like, "She isn't able to come to the phone right now. May I take a message?" Better yet, have your child screen calls on the answering machine.
- Your child should return messages promptly. Messages should be returned the same day if possible, the next day if not.

Making a Call

Most kids love to receive calls, but making a call can be intimidating even for the most outgoing child. Making a call doesn't have to be scary or difficult if you teach your child to follow these simple rules.

- Dial carefully.
- Speak clearly and at a normal speed. Your child should not mumble or talk so softly that others can't hear her.
- Your child should identify himself and ask for the person he wishes to speak with by saying, "Hello. This is Carl Warner. May I speak to Jennifer, please?" Saying, "*Can I* speak with Jennifer?" or "Is Jennifer there?" should be replaced with "*May I* speak with Jennifer, please?"
- Your child should use her full name when calling an adult or an acquaintance. She may use only her first name when calling a close friend or relative.
- When leaving a message on an answering machine or voice mail, teach your child to leave his name, phone

number, and a brief message. Answering machines are not for long messages or pranks.

- Your child should say "thank you" when someone takes a message for her.
- Make sure your child knows how to dial 911 in case of emergency. Also make sure your child knows his phone number as early as possible. Lost children as young as two or three years of age have been reunited with parents because they could remember their phone number.
- If your child dials a wrong number, she should say, "I'm sorry. I've dialed a wrong number." It is impolite to just hang up.
- Your child should ask permission before using another's phone.

Telephone Tips

- Your child should not make calls too early (before 8:00 a.m.), too late (after 9:00 p.m.), or during the dinner hour without permission.
- If you are a parent of a preteen or teenager, you know that the telephone has the potential to be your child's best friend and your worst nightmare. Set clear rules for telephone use. Allow your child to help you set these rules, taking into consideration time needed for homework, other family members' need for the phone, etc.
- Others are not to be disturbed when they are speaking on the phone. Teach your child that telephone time is time to respect the conversations of others. Do not allow your child to interrupt you except in case of emergency. If you have a small child, make every attempt to make or receive lengthy calls when your child is occupied, taking a nap, or watching a favorite video or DVD.

Small children can't and shouldn't supervise themselves. On the other hand, they must learn to respect your time on the phone; and as they get older, you must learn to respect their time on the phone as well.

- An older child can learn the various functions on a phone: speed dial, redial, call waiting, long distance versus local calls, etc.

Remember four-year-old Brooke with the incredible telephone manners? How did a four-year-old learn manners that could rival that of a corporate CEO? Simple—she practiced.

Before Brooke was allowed to begin answering the phone, her savvy mother pulled out an old toy phone and practiced with Brooke until she was ready. If you have a young child, practice with your child until she is capable of answering the phone correctly. Once your child feels confident, allow her to make or receive a call with your supervision.

If your child is already used to making and receiving phone calls, you may need to replace some bad habits. Make it a family event. Break some of your bad habits as well. Be sure to reward your child for good telephone manners. Who knows? Maybe the telephone will be the place for you and your child to "connect."

Cell Phones

Who hasn't been disturbed during a movie, church service, or important event by a ringing cell phone? While attending my son's back-to-school night, I was stunned to observe a parent answer his cell phone and carry on an entire conversation at full volume in the middle of a teacher's presentation—and he did so without the slightest indication of embarrassment or remorse.

Cell phones can be a blessing or a curse, depending on how they are used. To make sure you and your child use a cell phone properly, follow these simple guidelines.

- Your child should turn his cell phone off or set it on silent mode at church, movies, the library, and any place where others are trying to listen or concentrate.
- If your child receives a call while with another person, she should make her call brief or ask to return the call. She should not ignore a companion for the sake of a cell phone call.
- Teens should avoid using cell phones while driving. Some states have laws forbidding their use while driving due to the distractions they cause.
- Your child should return cell phone messages promptly, just as he would with a traditional phone message.

Email and Instant Messages

Remember when you couldn't believe your parents didn't have a VCR when they were kids? Well, our kids can't believe we didn't have Internet access.

We didn't. But they do. So it's important to know the rules of use for the computer age. An email is not as formal as a letter, not as casual as an instant message, but protocol still applies. Teach your child the following guidelines.

- Emails should be short and to the point.
- Remember that an email is never truly private. An email message can be forwarded to others, so your child should use caution in what she says.
- Your child should not use all capital letters when writing an email. Using all capital letters is equivalent to shouting a message.
- Your child should avoid "flaming," which is the use of foul language, dirty jokes, or anything that might offend the reader.

- While some people are beginning to use email to send invitations, it is still best to use traditional methods.

Instant Messages and Chat Rooms

If you have Internet access and a child over the age of twelve, you have probably encountered the wonders of instant messaging and chat rooms. An instant message is similar to talking on the phone. Messages move quickly back and forth from one person to another. The advantage (or disadvantage!) of instant messages and chat rooms is that many people can engage in conversation at one time.

The rules of email also apply to instant messages:

- brief messages
- no flaming
- avoid all capitalization

Because of the public nature of instant messages and chat rooms, it is extremely important for parents to monitor their children's use of this medium. What can begin as an innocent conversation between two kids can quickly become a stream of inappropriate language and content as friends of friends of friends join the conversation.

To avoid having your child exposed to inappropriate language, place your child's computer in a public area of your home. Never give your child access to the Internet in his room. Still, limiting Internet access to public spaces doesn't necessarily mean that monitoring his messages will be simple. Many parents complain that messages are difficult to decipher due to the intricate symbols and abbreviations used in messaging. To help you decode your child's Internet messages, the following is a list of common symbols and abbreviations used in emails, chat rooms, and instant messages.

136

Symbol/ Abbreviation	Translation	Symbol/ Abbreviation	Translation
: -)	smiley face/happy	FYEO	for your eyes only
;-)	wink	G/F	girlfriend
:-(	frown/sad	G2G or GG	got to go
:-0	yell	GR8	great
:-@	scream	HRU	How are you?
:-e	disappointment	IB	I'm back
:->	devilish grin	ILU or ILY	I love you
:-D	shock or surprise	JK	just kidding
:-P	wry smile	LD	later dude
:-Q	smoker	LOL	laugh out loud
:-!	foot in mouth	MOS	mother over shoulder
:-{	mustache	PLZ	please
:-&	tongue-tied	POS	parent over shoulder
:-	male	PRW	people/parents are watching
>-	female	PU	That stinks!
B/F	boyfriend	SPST	same place, same time
B4	before		
B4N or BFN	bye for now	SRY	sorry
BAK	back at keyboard	SUP	What's up?
BBL	be back later	THX or TY or TU	thanks or thank you
BF	best friend	WAYF	Where are you from?
BRB	be right back	W/B	write back
CU (or CYA)	see you (see ya)	WU	What's up?
EMA	email address		
F2F	face to face		

Connecting with others is as vital to our lives as breathing. Learning the right way to connect over the phone and Internet will help ensure your child's relational and professional success during his childhood, teenage years, and into adulthood. Follow the guidelines in this chapter to teach your child the proper way to handle these important "connections."

Training Schedule

Training Tips

1. Let a young child make a fun phone call (to grandma, a friend, or a favorite relative, perhaps).
2. Allow an older child to RSVP to a party he is invited to, call for pizza, or use 411 for directory assistance.
3. Let your child answer the phone this week, noting his telephone manners.

Manner I plan to teach:

How I plan to train:

Tools I will need:

Reinforcement I will use:

11

Week 5

Party Time in the Jungle

Chloe's twelfth birthday turned out to be more than either she or her mother bargained for. Born April 2, Chloe, with the help of her mother, Denise, decided on an "April Fools" theme to celebrate her birthday. Chloe and Denise giggled mischievously as they planned the funny pranks to be pulled on Chloe's party guests. But unbeknownst to Chloe, her mom had a few tricks up her sleeve to fool her daughter, as well.

On each invitation, Chloe's mom included a secret note for guests to bring a gag gift along with their birthday gift. As the guests arrived, Denise hid the regular gifts and placed the gag gifts alongside the cake for Chloe to open after games had been played and pranks had been pulled.

Excitedly Chloe began opening her gifts. First came a small box of breath mints. "Thank you very much," Chloe responded politely. Later she confessed to her mom that she figured the unusual gift was all her guest could afford and she didn't want to make her guest feel bad. Next came a gift from one of Chloe's closest friends. *Surely this will be something good,* Chloe thought. But to Chloe's surprise, her closest friend had gotten her a travel sewing kit, the kind hotels give away free alongside shampoo and conditioner.

"Thanks so much. I'm going to New York next month, and this will be perfect to take along," Chloe said sweetly.

Chloe sighed and continued opening her gifts. She politely thanked each guest for her thoughtfulness, never suspecting that an April Fool's joke had been pulled on her—until she peered inside a meticulously wrapped box that held, of all things, an old worn-out shoe covered in mud.

"OK, what's going on?" Chloe laughed.

"April Fools!" her guests shouted. Amazed with the success of their joke, Chloe's guests laughed for the rest of the afternoon. But her guests' parents were amazed at something else—Chloe's thoughtful manners.

"Can you believe how gracious Chloe was?" one mom commented.

"I know. I'm not so sure my daughter would have been so polite under the circumstances," said another.

Chloe's mom expected surprises at Chloe's April Fools birthday party. She just didn't realize what a nice surprise she would get too.

Everyone loves a party, but no one likes a child with bad party manners. As every parent knows, parties can bring out the best or worst in a child. Often overstimulated, overindulged, and overfed on candy, cookies, and cake, even the sweetest child can become a parent's worst nightmare without a little preparty preparation. This chapter will help your child have party manners worth celebrating.

Manners for Guests

RSVP

The letters RSVP stand for the original French request "Répondez, s'il vous plaît," which means, "Reply, if you please." When an RSVP is requested, you *should* respond, whether you plan to attend or not. Hosts use this important information to plan food, party favors, and other party essentials. To fail to RSVP is inconsiderate.

Parents should RSVP for their child until the preteen years. During later childhood your child can RSVP herself. She should know that all she needs to convey is her name and whether or not she will be able to attend the party. She should end the call by saying, "Thank you for inviting me."

Arrive and Leave on Time

Most hosts don't start games and activities until all children have arrived, so make sure your child arrives on time. If your child must be late, inform the host beforehand. Also, be sure to pick your child up on time. Be considerate of your host's schedule.

Come Prepared

Your child should arrive at a party prepared for whatever activity is planned. If the party is a sleepover, she should have her own sleeping bag, pillow, and toothbrush. If she is attending a swim party, she will need an appropriate bathing suit. Obviously, a birthday party requires a gift. For a young child attending her first sleepover, it is a good idea to send along any special toy or blanket she likes to sleep with. If you have any questions about party plans, ask the host in advance. As a parent, it is important to know the family with whom your child is staying. Before allowing your child to stay overnight at someone's home, you will want to be certain your child will be well cared for and well supervised.

Be a Good Sport

No child wants to be a party pooper, but when a child refuses to play party games or plays with a bad attitude, that's exactly what he is. Party games and activities are to be participated in with a positive, fun-spirited attitude no matter how silly or boring a child may think they are.

There is, however, one exception to this rule. If the game or activity is something your child feels morally uncomfortable participating in, then your child should refuse without feeling the least bit guilty about his unwillingness to participate. Talk with your child about possible scenarios beforehand. Your child should be aware of acceptable versus unacceptable movies he may view at a sleepover; he should be aware of acceptable versus unacceptable activities at boy-girl parties. Make sure your child knows he can call you at any time should a party get out of hand.

Say Something to Everyone

A party is the perfect time to mix, mingle, and make new friends. Often party guests do not all know each other. Some guests may be neighbors; some may be friends from school. Other guests may be friends from church or a sports team. It is the host's responsibility to introduce guests, but a socially savvy guest knows that she can make or break a party by how she relates to the other guests. A guest who talks only to her best friends makes others feel left out. Although it is great to have close friends, the rule of thumb when attending a party is to say something to everyone. Unless a party is unusually large, this is a do-able principle that ensures that everyone has a good time and no one feels isolated or alone. Parties should be fun for everyone.

Say "Please" and "Thank You"

When the energy level is high, the music is loud, and more than a few kids are thrown together, it is easy to forget good manners. Prepare your child before a party by reminding him to say, "Please," "Thank you," "Yes, please," or "No, thank you." Your child should remember to treat others' personal property with respect. This means no going through personal belongings, staying out of off-limits rooms, keeping feet off the furniture, no running inside the house, etc. Remind your child to thank his host and the host's parents when leaving the party.

Table Manners

The rules of good table manners apply to parties as well, with a few additions. At a birthday party, the birthday child should be the first to take a bite of birthday cake. Guests should not ask for a specific piece of cake. Kids, it seems, all want the same thing. So when little Camden asks for the piece with the rose on top, everyone else wants the piece with the rose on top too. Teach your child to accept what she is given with a polite "Thank you." If your child doesn't want the food offered, she should simply say, "No, thank you."

Be Willing to Play Second Fiddle

A party, especially a birthday party, is meant to honor the birthday child. It is his special day. Your child should be willing to allow the birthday child to be "star" for the day. This means the birthday child should choose activities, food, and so on, and the other children should willingly go along with his choices without complaint. Nothing can spoil a party faster than guests second-guessing a host's decisions or choices. Teach your child to put her own desires on hold for a few hours and focus her energy on making her friend's special day special. Odds are, she will have a great time and so will everyone else.

Manners for Hosts

A party is an especially exciting day for the host. But with the excitement also comes responsibility.

The Invitation

Party invitations should be received ten to fourteen days before a party. Christmas party invitations may be sent a bit sooner due to the busy nature of the season. If a guest receives an invitation too early, the event may be forgotten; too late, and her schedule may be filled. Ten to fourteen days gives a guest just about the right amount of time to plan to attend a party.

Generally, invitations should be mailed, although it is also acceptable to telephone an invitation. However, for clarity's sake, a written invitation provides a guest with all pertinent information—time, place, type of event. The details of an invitation extended by phone can be easily forgotten. If your child plans to include all her classmates, or just all of one gender, invitations may be given at school. However, if not all children are invited, it is wiser to mail invitations rather than risk hurting the feelings of an uninvited child.

More recently some people have opted to email invitations. Because an emailed invitation is less personal and has more of a mass appeal, emailing party invitations is discouraged for personal parties. However, email may be used for general parties, such as end-of-the-season sports team parties.

Invitations should include the date, beginning and ending time of party, type of party, any special instructions (wear a costume, bring a bathing suit, etc.), and address of the party. Directions are a nice addition. Include an RSVP number with a voice mail or answering machine to make the guests' job of responding easier.

As tempting as it may be, your child should never discuss her party in front of children who are not invited. This means no chatting about the big bash at the school lunch table or where others can overhear. Teach your child to be sensitive to the feelings of those around her.

The Big Day

- Both you and your child should be dressed and ready to greet guests thirty minutes prior to the party. This means decorations are in place, food is out, drinks are ready to be served, games are planned, and goody bags are prepared. This allows you and your child to relax and be ready to greet guests warmly as they arrive. If you are hosting a party at a place other than your home, plan on arriving no later than thirty minutes prior to the party.
- Your child should greet guests as they arrive. If your child is playing with other guests, she should stop for a moment, walk to the guest, offer to take the newcomer's coat, and introduce the person to the other guests. If the guest has brought a gift, your child should say, "Thank you," as she takes it and places it with the other presents. She should then offer her guest something to drink or a snack if available.
- The main responsibility for any host or hostess is to ensure that all guests have a good time. Helping your child make introductions and preparing your child to play or visit with every guest will help the party flow smoothly and allow everyone—host included—to relax and have fun.
- The birthday child should pass food to the guests before serving herself. Birthday cake, however, is served to the birthday child first. Guests should wait for the birthday child to take the first bite of cake before they begin to eat.
- At a birthday party, your child should open gifts fairly quickly, especially if he has numerous gifts to open. Have your child announce who the gift is from before he opens

145

it and thank the giver afterward. Your child should look at the giver as he offers his thanks. Each gift and each guest should receive a sincere "thank you," whether your child likes the gift or not. If your child receives duplicate gifts or receives a gift he already has, help him say something positive like, "Great minds think alike" or "Two is better than one." Your child should never show displeasure over a gift or say, "I'll take it back." Your child may exchange the present later if a gift receipt was provided with the gift.

- For a small child, there is nothing quite as exciting as receiving presents. Often very young children become so excited they help each other open presents! As long as this causes no distress for the birthday child, you may allow preschool-age children to pitch in and help.

Saying Good-Bye

The presents have been opened. The games have been played. The cake is gone. It's time to say good-bye. As guests leave, your child should excuse herself from whatever she is doing, walk the guest to the door, and thank her for coming. Of course, a guest should thank the host for having her and thank the host's parents as well.

Thank You Notes

Gifts are a tangible expression of love and friendship. A gift should be acknowledged with a verbal "thank you" and a written thank you note. The most important qualifications of a thank you note are that it be sincere, neatly written, and prompt—preferably delivered within one week after receiving a gift. The longer your child waits to write a thank you note, the easier it is to forget.

146

Thank you notes should be written on nice stationary, card stock, or thank you cards. Your child should use his best handwriting, although you don't need to be a stickler about perfection. Just make sure the writing is legible.

If your child is too young to write his own thank you notes, you will have to write them for him, but this doesn't mean your child cannot participate. Have your child draw a "thank you" picture or sign his name. Talk about the thoughtfulness of the giver. Let your child place the stamp on the envelope. Make writing thank you notes fun for your child.

How to Write a Thank You Note

- Begin with "Dear____."
- Thank the giver for the gift, naming it specifically.
- Tell why you like the gift or how you plan to use it, especially if the gift is money.
- Say something nice about the giver.
- End with "Love," "Your friend," or "Sincerely."

The length and complexity of your child's thank you note will vary depending on her age. A one-sentence thank you note is perfectly acceptable when written by a first grader. However, by fourth or fifth grade, your child should be able to master the basic components of writing a thank you note mentioned above.

> *Dear Grandma,*
>
> *Thank you for the twenty dollars you gave me for my birthday. I bought a new CD I have been wanting for months. I listen to it every day.*
>
> *I am so glad you were with me for my birthday dinner. You helped make my birthday extra-special!*
>
> *Love,*
> *Kelsey*

When to Write a Thank You Note

Your child should always write a thank you note . . .

- when she receives a gift by mail and is unable to thank the giver in person.
- when she stays with someone as a houseguest two or more nights

It is a nice idea for your child to write a thank you note . . .

- when she receives any type of present
- when she is a party guest
- when someone has shown your child special thoughtfulness

The Considerate Houseguest

When my husband was informed on short notice of an out-of-town job interview that required my presence as well, we scrambled to find friends who could keep our two kids, then ages five and two. Fortunately, a couple in our small group Bible study with two kids of their own volunteered to watch our children overnight.

We hurriedly packed our bags, rushed our kids to our friends' home, kissed them good-bye, and departed. It was the first time our two-year-old had been left overnight with anyone but her grandmother.

How did it go? You decide.

We arrived back home late the following evening, tired but excited to see our children. We thanked our dear friends profusely for their kindness and then inquired about the kids.

"How were they?" we asked.

"Taylor was an absolute angel," my friend Sheryl offered, conspicuously leaving out any information about our daughter.

"How about Kylie?" I prodded.

"Actually," she hesitated, and then went on, "I was debating whether I should mention this, but we had a bit of a hard time getting her to obey."

"Really? What happened?" I asked, my heart beating faster with dread.

"Well, when I put her down for a nap yesterday, she began kicking the walls with her heels. She really wasn't being naughty at that point, but when I asked her to stop so the other kids could go to sleep, she just kept on kicking. When I asked a second time, she looked at me and said, "I don't have to do what you say. You're not my mommy."

My heart dropped right to my toes.

"I'm so sorry," I lamely apologized. Truthfully, the phrase "Ignorance is bliss" sounded pretty good to me at that moment, but instead I added, "Thanks for telling me."

Granted, our daughter was only two years old, but the notion that she would speak to an adult with such disrespect floored us. She had never spoken to us that way, or to anyone else, as far as we knew. We wondered why she would do such a thing.

For a young child, being in someone's home overnight can be a scary, intimidating event that brings out all kinds of insecurities. Of course, this doesn't excuse poor behavior, but it can explain it. So as a parent who wants to ensure that your child behaves appropriately, you will want to make sure your child knows how to be a considerate houseguest.

Being asked to visit a friend or relative, whether for one night, one weekend, or one week, is one of the nicest compliments your child can receive. When your child follows the following guidelines, he will be sure to be a guest who gets invited back.

(By the way, our Kylie is now one of the nicest houseguests I know!)

The Overnight Bag

If your child is young, you will need to pack his overnight bag. During your child's preteen and teen years, he can pack his own. But whether you or your child does the packing, make sure your child arrives at his destination prepared. He should have his own toothbrush and other toiletry items, a change of clothes, including clean underwear, pajamas, and any other necessary items, such as a sleeping bag, bathing suit, pillow, or special blanket or toy. He should pack as lightly as possible while including everything necessary for his stay.

The Arrival

Once your child arrives at his destination, he should place his suitcase or overnight bag where the host designates. Make sure he knows to keep his bag in an out-of-the-way spot and keep his things together. Many kids are notoriously unorganized. Clothes, toys, and personal items can end up anywhere and everywhere if your child doesn't make an effort to keep his things in one spot. If his visit is longer than one or two nights, he may be given a place to unpack his clothes. If so, he should unpack in such a way that he will be able to find his things easily at the end of his visit.

If your child's stay is for a weekend or longer, he should bring a small gift for his host or hostess. The size of the gift will depend on the length of his stay. A box of gourmet cookies, a houseplant, or flowers are all nice gestures of thanks.

The Visit

- Your child should be ready, willing, and eager to go along with the customs and plans of the family he visits. Meals, activities, and schedules vary from family to family. When your child is a guest in someone's home, he should follow their lead without complaint.

- Your child should treat his host's home with respect. This means keeping things neat: making his bed in the morning, picking up toys and games, and leaving the bathroom clean (no hair in the shower, no wet towels on the floor, no water splashed around the counter). This also means no running inside the house, no snooping in drawers, looking in closets, or reading private mail.
- Your child should obey the host family's rules.
- If your child is served an unfamiliar food, he should take a little and try it. Some of your child's favorite foods may be meals he first tried at a friend's home. It is never polite for your child to say, "We never eat that" or "I don't like that."

The Departure

When your child leaves, he should thank both his friend and his friend's parents. A written thank you should be sent within one week if your child's stay was longer than one night. A thank you note should also be written for a one-night stay if your child was treated to something extra-special, such as a trip to an amusement park, the theater, or a professional sporting event.

"Wrapping It Up"

With a little practice and guidance, you can be sure your child will behave with kindness and consideration when visiting another's home, whether for a party or for a weekend stay. Teach your child good party manners and you both will have something to celebrate!

Training Schedule

Training Tips

1. Have a party—even an impromptu one! Let your child make homemade party invitations, call friends, or simply go door to door to invite neighborhood friends. Plan easy games, relays, or crafts. Older kids can go on a scavenger hunt.
2. If a birthday or holiday is just around the corner, allow your child to help plan the party. She can help decide the theme, decorations, food, games, or activities.
3. Before your child attends a friend's party, discuss proper party manners.
4. Have your child write a thank you note to someone who has done something thoughtful or helpful for him recently. Maybe a teacher, coach, friend, or family member would appreciate a note of thanks from your child.

Manner I plan to teach:

How I plan to train:

Tools I will need:

Reinforcement I will use:

12

WEEK 6

Swinging with the Other Monkeys

My heart broke as I listened to the muffled sounds of my nine-year-old son's sobs coming from behind his bedroom door. Our family's move meant leaving behind a classroom of friends and the security and comfort of two "best" friends he'd had since the age of three. Now alone and out of place, he found himself trying desperately to find a niche for himself after our midyear move.

I choked back my own tears. My heart hurt. I wanted to take him in my arms and run back "home" to the safety and security of people we knew and loved. I wanted to scream, "What's wrong with you—don't you see what a great kid he is?" to the classroom of kids currently ignoring him.

But I could do neither. When it comes to making friends, kids must forge their own way.

Nothing has the power to bless our children's lives quite like friendship. But what can be the source of great joy can also be the source of great pain. Though my son soon made wonderful friends and years have passed, remembering his dilemma still breaks my heart.

Childhood friendships come and go, rise and fall. Friends one day, enemies the next, children must learn the delicate balance of human relationships by navigating the sometimes rough waters of friendship.

So what's a parent to do? Are we left to merely observe our child's successes or failures in friendship? Not at all. While we can't make our children's friends for them, we can provide a positive context in which friendship can develop. We may not be able to direct the wind, but we can adjust the sails. We can teach our children the qualities necessary for being a good friend.

The acronym ALERT will help you and your child remember the qualities necessary for making and keeping friends.

A—Amiable

Generally speaking, nice kids have friends. Many kids, however, fall short at this very point. If a child relates with ease and can get along with others, he will be able to develop friendships. At a minimum, amiable kids speak to others when spoken to. But more frequently, amiable kids initiate relationships. They say, "Hi," to other kids at the park, at school, or on the field. They smile. They play fairly. They listen. They laugh. They know how to give and take. Amiable kids are pleasant to be around, which is why amiable kids make friends.

L—Loyalty

When asked to name important qualities of good friends, a group of my daughter's twelve-year-old buddies immediately piped up with "You can count on them"; "They don't talk behind your back"; "They stick with you." What these girls described is loyalty.

154

Kids who make and keep friends do so because they are not fickle—friendly one day and aloof the next. They do not talk badly about friends. They don't embarrass others by teasing or sharing private information. Amiable kids *make* friends. Loyal kids *keep* friends.

E—Encouraging

Several years ago we lived next door to the most encouraging kid I have ever known. He routinely cheered other kids on with comments like "Good job," "Way to go," or "Great shot" as the neighborhood kids played whatever game captured their attention at the moment. He wasn't silly, insincere, or gushy with his praise. He was simply an encouraging kid. Not surprisingly, he was also a kid with a lot of friends.

Encouraging people have friends because encouraging people live others-centered rather than self-centered lives. It's hard to dislike an encouraging person.

R—Respect

One of the great things about friendship is that it enables us to find others who are like us. It has been said that true friendship starts the moment one person says to another, "What? You too? I thought I was the only one!" But an often overlooked benefit of friendship is that it allows us to connect with people who are different from ourselves. Kids who treat other people, however similar or different, with value and worth behave with respect.

Respect can be shown in myriad ways: listening when someone speaks, appreciating different ways of doing things, following through with commitments made. These actions, to name a few, communicate respect. A child who treats others as valuable and worthy of respect will have friends.

Children who make friends not only treat others with respect, they also respect themselves. People—kids included—are

155

drawn to others who feel comfortable with themselves. When children respect themselves, they are able to set healthy relationship boundaries, negotiate conflict, and feel the freedom to venture out into new social venues.

T—Thoughtfulness

Bernard Meltzer, professor emeritus at the University of Chicago Law School, said, "You can make more friends in two months by becoming really interested in other people than you can in two years by trying to get other people interested in you." If a child can grasp this concept, a child can make friends.

Kids can learn to implement this principle by asking others questions about themselves. "Do you have any pets?" "What's your favorite sport?" "Where do you go to school?" Questions like these can be good conversation starters with which kids can find common areas of interest.

Good Friends Are . . .

Amiable
Loyal
Encouraging
Respectful
Thoughtful

Another practical way to cultivate thoughtfulness is to remember a friend's birthday or special event. Recently my daughter came home from school with scads of balloons tied to her backpack—all thoughtful gestures from friends who remembered her birthday. Asking about a friend's important gymnastics meet, football game, or musical concert also shows thoughtfulness. A simple "How did your game go?" or "Did you have fun at your concert last night?" communicates interest in the events of a friend's life.

Finally, treating a friend with good manners shows thoughtfulness. When a child remembers to offer his friend food or a drink, lets a guest go first or choose what game to play, he demonstrates thoughtfulness. Thoughtfulness cultivates the groundwork for friendship to thrive.

These five character qualities are essential to develop and maintain healthy friendships. If your child is inadequate in one or more of these areas, you need to be honest with your child and let him know that every behavior bears a consequence. Some behaviors, like the ones mentioned above, attract others. Some behaviors, however, repel others. If your child can pinpoint his own behavior, he has mastered the first step in being ALERT (amiable, loyal, encouraging, respectful, and thoughtful).

These qualities will need to be discussed again and again over the course of childhood. What your child seems to grasp one day will elude him the next. Learning to behave as an ALERT child takes time, practice, and direction from a caring parent. But an ALERT child is well on his way to smooth sailing when it comes to making friends.

"You can make more friends in two months by becoming really interested in other people than you can in two years by trying to get other people interested in you."

Ten Pitfalls to Friendship

Kids are funny. Sometimes they just have no clue.

Recently a neighbor's daughter came home from school distraught over the way she had been treated by one of her classmates. "Jason is so mean, Mommy," she complained. "He's not a very nice boy."

"What happened?" her mother inquired.

"He said I was sooooo gross."

"Well, what happened to make him say that?" her wise mother asked.

"Oh, I was just picking my nose."

When it comes to kids and manners, you can't assume anything. Even something as simple as picking your nose (or *not* picking your nose!) must be explained to a child.

It is important for kids to know the positive behaviors required to be a good friend. But sometimes kids learn best if they can pinpoint the not-so-positive qualities that drive others away. Pointing out negative behaviors can be tricky—you want to validate your child and her feelings but at the same time make her aware of ways her behavior might be irritating others. To make the discussion a bit easier, try talking about the following people types with your child. See if she knows anyone who fits these categories. Use these kid-friendly terms to point out behaviors that may need to be improved.

Doormat. This child has difficulty asserting his wants and needs. Often quiet or shy, he finds himself giving in to the whims and desires of other children, even when they differ from his own.

Bully. This child attacks others physically or verbally to gain control. A bully often finds himself in the center of fights or conflicts, most often initiating a conflict when things don't go his way.

King (or Queen) of the Jungle. "Bossy" best describes this personality type. He or she must always be in charge. Kings and Queens like to tell others what to do. You might hear a queen bee say things like, "If you don't play what I want to play, then I won't be your friend anymore."

Mr./Miss Loose Lips. Tell this child a secret, and it will be all over school by the end of the day. This kid can't be trusted to keep personal matters personal.

Backstabber. This child presents one image of friendship in your presence and another when you are absent. Backstabbers talk behind your back, join gossip, and spread rumors. Backstabbers are often fickle. One day they seem to be your best friend; the next day they act as if you barely exist.

Hotshot. "Show-off" best describes this child. He often brags and rarely allows anyone else to be the center of attention for more than a few moments.

Teaser. "I was just kidding" is a phrase often repeated by a teaser. Unfortunately, her teasing often embarrasses or hurts others' feelings. Her humor isn't funny, just cruel.

Miss/Mr. Eggshell. In opposition to the Teaser stands Miss/ Mr. Eggshell. This child is overly sensitive. He interprets most all personal comments as hurtful. In his view, the world is full of "mean" kids.

Brother Smother. This child smothers other kids with his possessive demeanor. "Brother smother" has difficulty sharing friends with others. He often gets his feelings hurt when a special friend wants to play with another child, even for a short period of time.

The Pie Crust Kid. "Flaky" best describes this kid. Often this child reneges on commitments because she is lazy, forgetful, indecisive, or fickle. But for whatever reason, friends soon learn this child can't be counted on.

Tips for Parents to Encourage Friendship

Besides discussing character qualities of a good friend, is there anything you as a parent can do to help your child develop positive friendships? Yes! Try some of the following tips.

- Set your child up for success. Provide your child with ample opportunities to play with other kids his own age when he is well rested and fed. Developmentally, a child does not actually play *with* another child until sometime between the ages of two and three. Until that time, your child will play *alongside* another child.
- Invite a new child to your house to play.

159

- Ask your child's teacher for help in choosing appropriate friends.

- Keep playdates to groups of even numbers. Two or four is best. Even the best of friends have difficulty playing in a group of three. No child wants to be the odd child out.

- Encourage your child to join a sports team, musical group, church youth group, dance team, or after-school club. Many children won't try the unfamiliar, so you may need to help your child choose an activity you feel she would enjoy.

- Make sure your child is not so overly committed in structured activities that he has no time to develop relationships. Kids need time to be kids.

- Give a shy or introverted child permission to be herself. Not all children will have truckloads of friends, or will want to.

- Give the children space to play, but stay within earshot so you'll know what is going on at all times. It's a good idea to have a "doors open" policy when kids are playing in their bedrooms. Never allow boys and girls to be in their bedrooms alone together.

- If conflicts arise, refrain from becoming involved too soon. Childhood conflicts are usually brief and easily forgotten. Learning to work through conflict teaches your child lessons in negotiation, compromise, and self-expression, vital skills necessary for all healthy relationships.

- Do intervene if a child is hit, bitten, or bullied. Also intervene if you sense the children are unable to resolve a conflict on their own. You can help by offering suggestions, such as "Why don't you take turns?" or "How about doing something you both like?" Sometimes a diversion, like offering a snack, can help.

- Keep first-time visits short. You want to provide enough time to see if the children "click" but don't want the hours to drag on if they don't.
- If your child has trouble sharing, put away special toys. Talk with your child about sharing before the visit. Let your child choose toys or games he feels comfortable sharing before his guest arrives.
- Often a shy child benefits from playing with a slightly younger child, which can give her the chance to be the leader. Shy children frequently feel more comfortable one-on-one rather than in large groups. Give your child ample opportunities to develop friends by initiating one-on-one playdates.
- If your child is bossy or has difficulty with other children, arrange to meet at a neutral place such as a park. For an older child who has difficulty with friends, an activity such as a movie, concert, or ball game can provide small amounts of interaction time, which can allow your child to have fun with other kids without putting undue stress on his limited social skills.
- Initiate "Park Days," "Pool Days," etc., open to all kids in your child's class.
- Teach your child assertiveness by allowing her to express her feelings and opinions at home. Make your home a safe place for all children to appropriately express their thoughts, ideas, and feelings.
- Always be prepared. Have a few activities, crafts, and suggestions in mind in case children can't agree on what to do.
- When your child visits a friend's home, pick your child up on time. No parent likes to be a free babysitter.
- Have your child help clean up any messes made during his visit.

161

- Treat your child's friend like you want your child to be treated, with kindness and consideration.

Good Sportsmanship

Fights among players on the field and among parents off the field have become common occurrences in today's society. Who would have thought that the sidelines of children's sporting events could become a breeding ground for violence?

In 2002 Thomas Junta was convicted of involuntary manslaughter in the beating death of Michael Costin at a hockey practice attended by sons of both men. Though an extreme example, unsportsmanlike conduct plays itself out in less dramatic ways across the playing fields of America every weekend.

At my own children's sporting events, I have witnessed boys spitting into their hands before shaking the opponents' hands; punches thrown on the sidelines; foul language spewed by players, fans, and parents; "trash talking" and temper tantrums. If you have kids in sports, you no doubt have witnessed your fair share of poor sportsmanship too.

To combat this epidemic, *you* must model good sportsmanship. You must also teach—and require—your child to behave with sportsmanlike conduct. Make sure your child knows the following rules of play.

Acceptable Behaviors

Your child should . . .

- arrive on time for all practices and games
- applaud during introduction of players, coaches, and officials
- remove his hat, face the flag, place his right hand over his heart, and remain still during the singing of the national

anthem; when singing, follow the lyrics of the national anthem precisely

- accept all decisions of officials
- listen to and follow instruction of coaches without complaint
- use positive, encouraging cheers only
- follow the rules of play
- shake hands with players after the game regardless of the outcome
- upon winning, shake his opponent's hand and say something encouraging like, "You played a great game"; be happy but don't gloat or brag
- upon losing, shake his opponent's hand, saying something nice like, "Good game." Of course your child will be sad or discouraged, but he should not be allowed to pout, complain, or blame others.

Unacceptable Behaviors

Your child should not . . .

- boo, yell derogatory remarks, or use foul language
- push or hit another player
- name call, laugh at, or criticize other players
- be a show-off or ball hog. He should be a team player, encouraging all his teammates to do their best. Remember: a team is only as good as its weakest link.

Behavior with the Opposite Sex

"Should I open the door for her?" "Will he pull out my chair for me?"

163

The lines of appropriate behavior between men and women have blurred over the last few decades, so perhaps it is more important than ever for kids to learn how to treat members of the opposite sex. Although the rules have changed, the principle behind them hasn't: kindness and courtesy never go out of style!

Members of the opposite sex should always be treated with respect. This means:

- no name calling
- no references to body parts
- no sexual jokes
- no whistles, catcalls, hoots, etc.
- boys hold doors open for girls and women. Help your son learn this nicety by having him hold the door open for his mother and sisters. Even a young school-age boy can do this. Don't forget to thank him and praise his courtesy.
- boys hold chairs out for girls and women. Have your son practice at nice restaurants or formal family dinners.
- boys allow girls and women to go first

Friendship has the power to enrich your child's life. By being an ALERT kid (amiable, loyal, encouraging, respectful, thoughtful) equipped with the tools for developing friends, your child will be on his way to developing meaningful relationships not only during his childhood, but also throughout his life.

Training Schedule

Training Tips

1. Drive your child and a friend somewhere this week. Don't talk—just listen. Observe how your child interacts

with peers. You may learn a thing or two about your child.

2. Read the ALERT section above with your child and discuss it.

3. Read your child the "not-so-positive" friendship styles mentioned in this chapter. Ask your child if he knows anyone who fits these categories. Does that child have friends? What does your child think of these types of behaviors? Does your child think he sometimes behaves in any of these ways? Ask your child how he thinks he could handle himself more positively.

Manner I plan to teach:

How I plan to train:

Tools I will need:

Reinforcement I will use:

13

PUTTING IT ALL TOGETHER
What to Expect and When

When it comes to training a well-mannered child, the most frequently asked questions center around *when* a child should be taught manners. Parents wonder "Is it too late?" or "Is it too early?" Almost as critical as knowing which manners to impart is knowing when to impart them.

Part of training children to have good manners is knowing what behaviors to expect and when. Often parents expect too much or too little from their children, which causes frustration on the part of parent and child. In an effort to make your job as a parent easier, this chapter outlines the specific manners discussed throughout this book and spells out at what age parents can expect mastery of these skills.

The Toddler Years—Ages One to Three

Ages twelve to thirty-six months refer to the toddler years. And although still young, a child this age can begin to grasp the fundamentals of mannerly behavior. In fact, when a parent instills the basics early on, her job of raising a polite child becomes easier as the child matures. During these critical years a child can:

- begin to learn conversation skills
- learn "please" and "thank you"
- follow simple instructions
- learn "OK"
- begin to understand turn-taking and sharing
- develop the fundamentals of responsible behavior
- express gratitude
- learn to respect things
- incorporate basic table manners
- meet and greet others

Conversation Skills

Speak to your baby from her earliest days. Babies and toddlers who are frequently spoken to develop social and verbal skills more rapidly than children who are not frequently spoken to. When you chat with your child while changing her diaper, driving in the car, or doing household chores, you impart the foundations of social conversation. Your child begins to internalize the subtleties of polite behavior, such as tone of voice, facial expressions, and word choice by listening to you speak to her. More important, when you speak to your child, you communicate your love for her and her value in your eyes. Through these earliest interactions, your child begins to develop her sense of self-worth and concept of acceptable social behavior.

Communicate with your child beginning in infancy and continue throughout childhood. Parents who freely talk with their children during their early years will be more likely to experience open communication with their children during the all-important teenage years.

Please and Thank You

You should begin to teach your child to say "please" and "thank you" as soon as he begins to speak. Let's say your eighteen-month-old child sees a banana on the kitchen counter. Unable to say "banana," he points and grunts to communicate his desire. You can help him learn polite behavior by saying something like, "Would you like the banana? Say 'banana, please,'" as you hand him the banana. Repeat the words "thank you" as you give your child the banana. Of course, at twelve to eighteen months, your child probably won't be able to say "please" or "thank you," but he will begin to comprehend that his desires and the words "please" and "thank you" go hand-in-hand.

By the time your child is three, "please" and "thank you" should be part of his everyday vocabulary. You may still have to remind your child to use these words, but as he nears the end of his third year, your reminders should be less frequent. If your child does not say "please" and "thank you" by this point, make sure you are not rewarding your child by giving in to his desires before he asks with a polite "please."

Follow Simple Instructions

Isn't it funny that even before a child can speak, she somehow knows exactly what you are saying? She may not be able to say the word *toy*, but hearing the word brings a smile to her face.

During the toddler years, your child is ready to learn to follow simple instructions. This skill forms the foundation on which respect for other people and other things is built. Your child should learn to follow your instructions to "come" and to "stop." She should also begin to understand the meaning

169

of the word *no*. The ability to follow these instructions not only prepares her to become a respectful child, it could also save her life.

A child who has been taught to follow her parents' instructions will be kept from untold harm when she wanders too close to a pool, too near the street, or too close to any number of other dangers. A child who stops when you say, "Stop," comes when you say, "Come here," or doesn't touch when you say, "No," will be spared from many a childhood disaster.

The best way to ensure that your child learns to do what you say is to teach her to say, "OK, Mom," or "OK, Dad," in answer to your instructions. Role-play this response. Remind your child. And reinforce this behavior. The importance of learning to follow instructions cannot be overstated. Everything else your child learns from her parents, teachers, coaches, and bosses will depend on her ability to follow instructions.

Sharing and Turn-Taking

During your child's toddler years, you will introduce sharing and turn-taking. As every parent knows, the word *mine* quickly becomes a favorite of every child over the age of one. Don't fret if your one- to two-year-old struggles with the concept of sharing; it's to be expected. Babies and young toddlers have little concept of where their things end and others' things begin. Don't take it personally if your twelve-month-old takes a toy out of another child's hand or if another child takes a toy out of your child's hand.

Do, however, begin to stress the importance of sharing during these years. Instruct your child to give back a toy he takes without asking. Help your child play fairly. Teach your child to wait his turn. By the age of three, these acts can be understood, even if not always applied.

Responsible Behavior

Even during the toddler years, children can develop a sense of responsible behavior. Kids this age love to "help" with chores. Permit them to do whatever their age and interest level allows. Between one and a half and two years of age, the concept of picking up their things can be introduced. Begin by having your toddler "help" you put away her toys, clothes, books, and other personal items. Gradually allow her to do these tasks more independently. By the time a child ends her third year, she should be able to put away her own toys, put her dishes on the counter, put away crayons, and so on.

Express Gratitude

While a toddler can't write a thank you note, he can learn to express gratitude when he "helps" you by drawing a picture on a thank you note you write for him. Begin discussing the importance of being thankful for what we have, what we receive, and for the people in our lives.

Learn to Respect Things

Your home should be a kid-friendly, child-safe environment during your child's infancy and toddler years. Latches on cabinets; household cleaners and medicines out of reach; dangerous objects removed—these precautions should be givens. However, it is simply impossible to remove every item your toddler should not touch.

Instead, teach your child to respect things. Do not allow her to rummage through Grandma's purse when she comes to visit. Don't allow her free access to siblings' rooms and personal items. You will need to say, "No, no," when she attempts to touch others' belongings. You may need to redirect, distract, or discipline your child in other appropriate ways to help her learn to respect others' things.

Table Manners

It will be many years before your child fully grasps all the intricate concepts of fine dining, but the fundamentals of table manners begin during your child's first year. From one to three years of age, your child should learn to wash hands before coming to the table, stay seated while eating, and use a bib and later a napkin. During these years your child will also begin to use silverware. Your focus now should be on helping him get his spoon to his mouth. How he holds his silverware is not an issue for the toddler. However, when your child is between two and three years of age, you may begin to teach him the proper way to hold his spoon and fork, although developmentally this may take some months to master.

Meeting and Greeting Others

From ages one to three, your child can learn to meet and greet others by saying, "Hi" and "Bye-bye," and learning to wave. As your child ends her third year, you will want to introduce the concept of saying, "It's nice to meet you," when she meets an adult.

Children this age vary greatly in how they respond to meeting new people. Some children never seem to meet a stranger; others bury their heads in their parents' shoulders or hide behind their legs. Your main job during these years is to model good manners when meeting others. You may introduce your child by saying, "This is my son, Jonathan," and then proceed with your adult conversation.

Allow your child to see you respond with kindness and consideration to those you meet.

Learning to Love God

It's never too early to begin to teach your child about God and his love. I have found that the quiet moments before bedtime provide some of the most precious moments to discuss God's love and provision with my child. Try reading a Bible written specifically with toddlers in mind at bedtime. The stories will be short and simple and will impart the timeless truth of God's love and his plan for our lives. Toddlers don't have to be convinced of a God who loves them; they have a simple faith that pleases the Lord. Your child's faith may very well increase your own!

From the time your child is born, pray daily for her. If the idea of prayer seems foreign to you, simply express your concerns for your child to God honestly and sincerely. Remember, God is not as concerned with our words as he is with our hearts. Allow your child to hear you pray for her. What a sense of security a child has when she hears Mom or Dad pray for God's blessings and protection over her!

Both my husband and I have prayed with all three of our children as we tuck them into bed at night. When they were infants, I stood over their cribs rubbing their backs as I whispered a prayer for their safety and God's blessing and direction in their lives. As they grew, we continued our nightly ritual of bedtime stories and prayers. Soon they began praying simple prayers on their own. By the time they reached three years of age, each child firmly embraced God's love and tender affection for them. It's never too early to teach your child the life-transforming truth of God's love.

The toddler years are full of wonder and myriad new learning opportunities for the twelve- to thirty-six-month-old child. Introduce the concept of mannerly living with a fun, positive, "this is just the way things are done" kind of attitude, and you will be well on your way to taming your family zoo and raising a well-mannered child.

The Preschool Years—Ages Three to Five

By age three your baby has become a child. From the ages of three to five, your child's world of social, intellectual, and physical development expands at a mind-boggling rate. Whereas his favorite thing to say during the toddler years was "mine," his favorite question during his preschool years will be "Why?" You can use his natural curiosity to your advantage as you begin to explain the "whys" behind good manners.

All you taught during your child's first three years will be reinforced and expounded upon during the next season of his life. However, he is now ready to learn more skills. During your child's preschool years he can:

- meet and greet others
- learn acceptable public behavior
- improve table manners
- develop friendship skills
- begin to answer the telephone properly
- learn party manners

Meet and Greet Others

From the ages of three to five, your child will likely be thrust into many new social situations. Her circle of friends and acquaintances will enlarge as she enters preschool, begins dance or music lessons, or joins sports teams—all for the very first time. During these years you may begin to teach your child how to formally respond when being introduced. A three-year-old will be able to say, "Hi," or better yet, "Hi, Miss Smith," when introduced to her preschool teacher. But it may not be until your child approaches her fifth or sixth birthday that she can remember to look an adult in the eye, shake hands, and say, "It's nice to meet you."

Learn Acceptable Public Behavior

Imparting acceptable versus unacceptable public behavior will be one of your biggest jobs during the preschool years. Now old enough to walk instead of ride in a stroller, the world can become a virtual playground for the three- to five-year-old child. Your child must learn when to run and when to walk, when to use a loud voice and when to use a quiet one, when to stay by your side and when to roam free. These years are the time to guide your child when using personal and public property.

Improve Table Manners

Your child has now moved from a high chair into a booster seat and sits with the rest of the family at the dinner table. It's time to begin teaching table manners. Your child should already know to wash his hands before eating, and he can use a fork and spoon, but his skills can now be expanded upon.

From the ages of three to five, your child can learn to hold a fork and spoon properly, help you set the table, clear his own dishes, place his napkin in his lap, keep his elbows off the table, and chew with his mouth closed. He should be instructed to ask for food by saying, "Pass the potatoes, please," not "I want more potatoes." He should also know to decline food by saying, "No, thank you," rather than "Yuck" or "I hate that." A preschool-age child can sit still while the family eats, ask to be excused before leaving the table, and say "thank you" to the person who made the meal.

When dining in a restaurant, your child is now old enough to know food is for eating, not for playing with. He should be required to sit until everyone has finished their meal and is ready to leave. It is a good idea to keep crayons and paper handy to keep your preschool-age child occupied when dining out. If your child becomes unruly, do not allow him to roam free, even by your table. This distracts other diners and sends the message that your child can get what he wants if he makes life difficult enough. Instead, remove your child. Let him know that impolite behavior in public is unacceptable. Dining with preschool-age children has its challenges, but when children learn acceptable table manners early, they are a pleasure later on.

Develop Friendship Skills

From the ages of three to five, friendships begin to be forged. In fact, as I write this, my seventeen-year-old son is visiting with one of his best friends who now lives an hour and a half from our home. When did they become "best friends"? On the first day of three-year-old preschool!

Kids this age have distinct personalities, likes, and dislikes. They get a sense of the kind of person they "connect" with and the kind of person they don't. At this age sharing and turn-taking can become cemented in your child's way of relating. Whereas these behaviors were mere concepts before, the three-to five-year-old can understand and implement them—though not always perfectly.

Kids this age can learn to develop empathy for others, show kindness and consideration to guests, and play fairly. During these years teach your child to let guests go first, to include outsiders in play, and to follow rules of fairness. Help your child work through childhood disagreements by offering suggestions, such as, "Why don't you let Sarah go first this time and you can go first the next." Teach your child to be a considerate guest in others' homes by having her help put away toys or games, asking by saying "please" and "thank you," and by treating others' property with care.

Telephone Manners

Your child will probably not be ready to answer the telephone properly until he approaches his fifth birthday. Before that time most kids view the telephone as nothing more than an interesting toy. At the age of three or four, your child can, however, learn the importance of dialing 911 in case of emergency. Just be sure he knows that 911 is to be reserved only for emergencies.

During his fourth or fifth year, you will want to introduce proper phone manners. Teach him to answer the phone with a polite "Hello" or "Hello. This is the Smith residence." For safety reasons, he should not give his name, nor should he ask, "Who is this?" If the call is for your child, instruct him to say, "This is Kelsey." If the call is for another member of your family, he should say, "One moment please," and then go get that person.

A child of four or five should ask permission before making a call. Teach him to dial carefully and to speak slowly and clearly. Children tend to rush their words out of excitement or mumble out of fear. Your child should ask for the person he wishes to speak with by saying, "May I speak with Kurt, please?" rather than "Is Kurt there?"

Party Manners

With your child's new social network, parties will no doubt begin to fill her social calendar—and yours too. When your child is between ages three and five, you will want to introduce good party manners. She should greet the host and the guests with a friendly "Hello" or "Hi"; play party games with a positive attitude; thank guests for their gifts; use good manners with adults; remember to say "please" and "thank you"; include all guests, exclude no one; and say "thank you" at the party's conclusion. At four or five, a birthday child can also sign her own name on thank you notes. A three-year-old can draw a picture on thank you notes or help you place stamps on the envelopes.

The preschool years are exciting years full of new experiences and rapid learning. Capitalize on your child's natural interest in the world around her by teaching her the basics of good manners during these years.

The Childhood Years—Ages Six to Twelve

Your child is off and running! Away from your supervision many hours of the day, he has his own network of friends and acquaintances. His ever-increasing sphere of relationships—teachers, coaches, neighbors, classmates, and friends—requires a certain proficiency in social skills. It is vital for your child to grasp the basics of good manners during his childhood years. As these common courtesies become part of the way your child relates to others, he will become a confident, thoughtful person and a joy to be around.

During these years your child can be expected to:

- improve and refine table manners
- learn good sportsmanship
- develop friendship and social skills
- make and receive calls competently
- write thank you notes
- set the table
- learn to make introductions

Table Manners

Your child is now ready to improve and refine her table manners. During her childhood years, she should learn to consistently chew with her mouth shut, keep elbows off the table, use a napkin correctly, and sit properly at the table. She should also be able to set an informal table. At around age seven or eight, your child can begin to learn to cut her own food using a knife. Because this ability depends largely on your child's fine motor skills, it may take some months before your child actually masters cutting her own food.

During these years you will want to teach your child the rules of formal dining as well. She can learn where the salad fork, soup spoon, and dessert silverware are placed. She should know the fundamental rule of silverware use: "Work from the outside in toward your plate."

Between the ages of six and twelve, your child should be able to sit quietly while dining in a restaurant. She should be able to order for herself and use proper table manners.

Good Sportsmanship

Most children become involved in some sort of athletics during their childhood years. From the ages of six to twelve, your child should understand the rules of his chosen sport and follow these rules without exception. He should be respectful to his coaches and teammates. He should be on time for practices and come prepared with any equipment necessary. Your child should be ready to finish a season he begins, knowing that a team depends on the reliability and faithfulness of every team member.

Friendship

Your child will likely develop many new friends during her childhood years. She should know how to be a good listener as well as a loyal friend. She should internalize a sense of fair play and sharing. During these years she may experience the disappointment that comes from choosing less than ideal playmates. Help your child choose her friends wisely by giving her frequent exposure to positive kids, perhaps children from church or children whose parents you know and respect.

During these years she will also begin to stay longer at friends' houses, unsupervised by you. She will probably have her first sleepover and may spend the night with numerous families during these years. She should be able to follow the family rules of her host's home; treat her host, host's parents, and host's home with respect; and be a courteous houseguest.

Phone Calls

Toward the end of your child's childhood years, the phone will probably become his best friend. He should know how to make and receive phone calls properly. He should also be able to take, as well as leave, phone messages. When taking a message, your child should repeat the caller's name and phone number to make sure he has copied it accurately. If your child has a cell phone, he should be familiar with cell phone manners.

Thank You

Your child is now old enough to write her own thank you notes. The length and complexity of these notes will depend on your child's age. A one-sentence thank you is fine for a first grader. By the time your child is in third grade, she will probably be capable of writing three- to five-sentence notes. By the fifth or sixth grade, your child should be able to write a fully developed thank you note and address it as well.

Making Introductions

Between the ages of six and twelve, your child will begin to feel comfortable meeting people of all ages. When your school-age child meets an adult, he should know to stand up, shake hands, make eye contact, smile, and say, "It's nice to meet you." Your child is now old enough to learn how to properly introduce others. He should learn how to introduce both peers (Molly, this is my friend Shannon) and adults (Mrs. Black, I would like you to meet my mother, Mrs. Hart).

180

The bulk of your child's foundational learning, both academic and social, occurs during the childhood years. Help set your child on the right course by ensuring that she becomes well acquainted with the social tools and polite behaviors necessary for relational success.

The Teenage Years—Ages Thirteen to Eighteen

Your years to impart your values are numbered. Your child is a teenager.

Though he may not realize it, your child needs you now as much as ever. Three parts child, one part adult, your child must negotiate the sometimes awkward years of adolescence. During your child's teenage years, you may notice some regression in his mannerly behavior from time to time. This is to be expected but not accepted. Now is the time for your child's manners to be refined, not misplaced. Manners for the teenager can be a welcome asset with dating and job interviews just around the corner. During these years your child should:

- treat the opposite sex with respect
- speak respectfully and confidently with adults
- master fine-dining skills
- practice good sportsmanship
- be conscientious in personal responsibilities

Opposite Sex

The key word for relating with members of the opposite sex is respect. Teenagers should treat one another with the consideration they would want shown themselves. They can show their consideration by calling at appropriate times, being on time for dates, and avoiding negative or inappropriate talk.

Speak with Adults

By the time your child is a teenager, she should greet adults she knows using their names (e.g., "Hi, Mr. Jones") and confidently shaking hands. She should be able to carry on a polite conversation with an adult, maintaining eye contact and speaking clearly. Although older and hopefully more confident than a few years prior, she should continue to maintain respect for adults.

Table Manners

During your child's teen years, he should master the basics of eating properly. Although you may have to remind him to take his elbows off the table, sit up straight, and stop drinking out of the juice pitcher, he should be fairly proficient in table manners. He should use a napkin without a reminder, chew with his mouth closed, and cut his food properly. While eating, he should sit with both feet on the ground.

You will now want to include your child in your fine-dining experiences. Allow your child to accompany you to nice restaurants from time to time. The more exposure he has to formal dining, the more relaxed and comfortable he will be in these settings in his adult years.

Now is the time to teach your child how to set a formal table. He should know where to find his bread plate, where his salad plate is located, and on which side he can find his salad fork and soup spoon. You may also want to teach him how to eat more difficult foods like crab, lobster, or artichokes.

Good Sportsmanship

Athletics can become fiercely competitive during the teen years. Sports your child and her peers once played for fun, they now may play for potential college scholarships. Sometimes the higher skill level, time commitment, and competition can provoke unsportsmanlike conduct. Your child should continue to abide by the rules of fair play. She should maintain respect for her coaches and teammates, and you should make sure to encourage these behaviors. Do not allow your child to exhibit a bad attitude toward coaches, teammates, or opponents on or off the field, even if you think her attitude is justified. Help your teenager compete with class.

Personal Responsibility

As your teen ages, privileges will increase; he will learn to drive, stay out later, and make more individual choices. But with privilege comes responsibility. By the time your child reaches the teenage years, he should bear the responsibility of caring for his personal commitments. This means he should complete homework, take care of personal household chores, and follow through responsibly with outside jobs. A teen may need help, encouragement, reminders, and more than a little prodding from time to time, but generally speaking, he must take ownership of his personal responsibilities.

The teenage years don't have to be feared. They can be fun! Your child's unique personality is now in full bloom. Her verbal skills, sense of humor, and intellect are becoming more on par with your own. Despite the inevitable rocky roads caused by hormonal changes and teenage dramas, living with a teenager, especially one who has been taught the value of kindness and consideration for others, can be one of life's greatest rewards.

14

QUESTIONS AND ANSWERS

Q: My first two children, a girl and a boy, are only thirteen months apart. People said constantly, "They'll be best friends!" Alas, it was not to be. They are now eight and nine, and the rivalry between them is the worst I've ever seen. They tattle on each other constantly, fight over the coveted space on the couch, and even count the number of crackers (or whatever) they are given to make sure they have the same amount. Their fighting creates a lot of stress for the entire family. Do you have any recommendations for us?

A: Sibling rivalry certainly does cause stress in a home. Of course, a certain amount of sibling rivalry is to be expected. Children argue from time to time—that's just life. An excessive amount of arguing, however, means that some changes are in order. First, examine the atmosphere of your home. Is it loving and positive? When a mom sets the tone of the home with loving affection and positive words with both her husband and her children, the amount of arguing diminishes.

That said, even in the most loving homes, kids who are close in age may still go toe to toe with one another. To help alleviate this tension, make sure each child is getting enough personal attention and has sufficient personal space. Also, sit down with your kids and have a heart-to-heart talk with them regarding their arguing. Ask them why they think they argue so much and if they like life better when they are getting along or when they are fighting. Help them see the value in cooperating rather than competing. Also, let them know that you won't tolerate the tattling and bickering anymore.

When the bickering between my own kids becomes excessive, I warn them one time. After that I make them stop whatever they are involved in and go to a room that they are not allowed to leave until their conflict is resolved. I have found that when I don't become emotionally involved in their disputes but simply dole out consequences while staying emotionally neutral, they have learned to settle their own disagreements and I have maintained my sanity.

Q: Why do we constantly have to use a "trigger" like "What's the magic word?" to get our boys to say "please" when they want something?

A: A big part of teaching children manners is reminding. As much as we would like our kids to grasp good manners the first time we teach them, life just doesn't work that way. I think it helps to realize that it is OK to remind your kids; just make sure you do it in a positive way. Also, make a special effort to reinforce polite behavior by noticing when your children do say "please" without your reminder.

In addition, an effective way to teach your children to say "please" without being reminded is to ignore their requests until they say "please." Sometimes parents inadvertently train their kids to rely on verbal prompts rather than taking ownership for polite behavior themselves. Ignoring impolite requests may provide the motivation your boys need to say "please" without being reminded.

Reminders are a vital part of the learning process, but by the time a child is school age, words like "please" and "thank you" should be pretty much mastered without your help.

Q: How can I get my ten-year-old boy to sit squarely on the chair at the dinner table and not on the edge, ready to roll as soon as supper is done?

A: For an active ten-year-old, eating is simply a utilitarian event. Open mouth. Insert food. Mission accomplished.

To help your son improve his table manners, make sure he knows *why* he needs to pull his chair to the table and sit forward (i.e., so food won't spill, because you want to be able to talk to him during dinner). Also, tell your son you will be watching how he sits at dinner (have this conversation apart from a meal) and praise whatever he does correctly.

Q: **Young girls today say that it is now not only socially acceptable for a girl to phone a boy, but if they are special friends, it is expected. My niece says if a guy calls a girl and she never reciprocates, he takes that as a "not interested" cue. From her perspective it is unfair to expect the guy to do all the phoning and initiating. The guys she knows hate phoning and find it hard if they are expected to always be the "vulnerable" one. At the risk of condoning "chasing guys," can you tell me about the current etiquette concerning girls phoning their male friends in general? What about a special male friend?**

A: In today's society it is more acceptable for teenage girls to call guys. However, many girls today are becoming overly aggressive. What they don't realize is that boys still do want to lead the way. It is OK for a teenage girl to call a guy she knows well periodically. However, girls need to realize that, in general, a teenage boy's need to chitchat is much less than a girl's. As a parent of a teenage boy, I know from personal experience that parents do not appreciate a girl who calls too frequently and neither does the boy.

So, bottom line: it is acceptable for teenage girls (not younger) to call boys they are close friends with as long as they don't overdo it.

Q: **How can I get my preschooler to chew with her mouth shut?**

A: Make learning manners fun by showing your preschooler why she should chew with her mouth shut. Chew with *your* mouth open and ask her how it looks. Explain that people don't like to eat with others who "gross them out." Play a game to see who can chew with her mouth shut most, and reward her with lots of praise. Realistically, you may need to remind her for at least several months—if not years! Try to make your reminders neutral. With one of my daughters, I simply put my finger to my lips as our secret signal that she was chewing with her mouth open. We found this to be a helpful method to teach her to chew with her mouth closed.

Q: **How do I teach my children good table manners when their father starts eating as soon as he is seated and often reaches into a dish on the table with his own fork? I have tried to talk to him about it to no avail. He gets angry and resentful and refuses to change. Help!**

A: You are not alone in your dilemma. Truthfully, you can't (and probably shouldn't) do anything about your husband's manners. But you can help your kids. It is important for kids to know the reasons behind good manners. For example, if they know that you place your napkin in your lap to avoid spills or use a serving fork instead of your own fork to avoid spreading germs, they will embrace manners a bit more easily. But when it comes to learning manners, practice is the most effective method. Just try to make dinnertime fun, with good conversation and neutral reminders. Direct any corrections toward your children, not your husband. Openly praise your children when they exhibit good manners. We all respond more favorably to praise rather than criticism, so keep learning fun and positive. Your whole family—husband included—is sure to benefit.

Q: **What is an effective way to get a toddler to look in your eyes when you are trying to discipline him or redirect his actions?**

A: How wise you are to start teaching your child early! A twelve-month-old will be distracted very easily, so don't fret too much if he has trouble focusing. But you are right in wanting him to look at you when you are disciplining or redirecting. The best way to get a small child to look at you is to say, "Adam, look at me." If he doesn't, gently take his face in your hands and turn his head toward you. To make eye contact easier, get down on his level when you really need him to focus on what you are saying. You don't want to get into a giant power struggle, but your child does need to pay attention to what you say.

Q: **I have a twelve-year-old daughter whose manners are atrocious. She chews with her mouth open, talks with her mouth full, takes large bites of food, and eats very fast. We tried as she was growing up to teach her good table manners, but she insists that her manners are not that bad. I'm not sure what to do. Is**

there any hope left? Note: I use subtle hand signals to gesture to her when she is doing something wrong in public, but many times it is either too late or goes "unnoticed."

A: You are certainly not the only mom with this problem. The key to teaching your daughter manners lies in something you said: "She insists that her manners are not that bad." She isn't motivated to change her behavior because she doesn't perceive that there is a problem. Your job is to motivate her to want to improve. The trick is to do this without being a nag. (Easier said than done, I know!)

To your advantage, your daughter is about to enter her teen years, during which how she is perceived will matter. You might try pointing out other kids' bad manners (at a restaurant, the mall, etc.) and ask what your daughter thinks about them. If she can *see* how bad manners look, she might be more motivated to improve. Pray for these teachable moments.

A big part of teaching manners is reminding kids to do what they have been taught. Your hand signal method is a great tool. Keep at it. Also, try making manners an agenda at the dinner table without being critical. The last thing you want is for your dinner table to be a battlefield. You might say, "Who has their napkin in their lap?" before your family starts to eat. Or "Who's chewing with their mouth closed?" and then proceed with conversation as normal.

Finally, if your daughter's manners are really atrocious, you may need to have a private heart-to-heart talk explaining that you want the best for her and never want her to be embarrassed or feel a lack of confidence. Now that she is getting older, you want to help her be the best she can be—and that includes learning manners. Help her see how learning manners will benefit her now and in the long run.

Q: **Are "rewards" good for children when they learn an etiquette task well? What kind of rewards would relate to the table?**

A: Learning any task is easier if positive reinforcement is used—table manners included! Praise is my favorite "reward," but other rewards are fine too. A game my family plays from time to time is the "penny (or nickel or dime) game." Each person in our family is given a certain number of pennies set beside his or her plate at dinner. During dinner, if another family member catches you using poor manners, he or she gets to take a penny away from you. However, if you are caught displaying a good manner, you can earn pennies. My husband and I make sure we are very

189

generous with catching our kids' good behavior, because the kids are pros at catching each others' bad behavior! This game is fun, but it dominates the dinner table, so you won't want to play it every night.

In regard to other rewards, stickers are a good option for young children. But for older kids, a special breakfast, lunch, or dinner date at the restaurant of their choice can be a great motivator. Just be specific as to what behavior must be mastered consistently in order to receive this reward. Then follow through by taking only this child on a special "date." It will be a treat for you and for your child!

Q: How important is it for children ages four to six to answer back to adults when greeted? No matter how much we practice, when the time comes, my kids seem tongue-tied.

A: It is very important for children to learn to greet adults when being introduced. But when children are four or five years of age, adults can be intimidating for children. The best course of action is to practice at home (which it sounds like you are already doing), especially immediately before your child will be in a situation where he is likely to meet others. Make sure your child feels comfortable practicing with you—it should be fun! Help him see how grown-up and impressive he will be when he smiles and says, "Hello." (At this age, a smile and a "Hello" or "Hi" will suffice.)

If your child still has trouble, simply whisper something like, "What do you say?" to remind him. If he still refuses to say, "Hello," simply proceed with your conversation. You don't need to make comments like "He's shy," which stereotype your child. Later, however, you will want to talk to him about why he wouldn't say, "Hello." Ask him what you can do to help make it easier for him. Maybe he will respond to a secret signal of his own choosing.

By the time your child is school age, he should be able to acknowledge an adult with a smile and a polite "Hello, it's nice to meet you." During the elementary age years (beginning around first grade), you will also want to teach your child to stand, shake hands, and look adults in the eye when introduced. It will take several practices for your child to become accustomed to doing all this correctly, but make sure he knows it is an important way for him to show respect for adults as well as a fun part of growing up!

Q: **What is an appropriate age to expect good manners in a restaurant environment? How can I encourage good manners at a restaurant?**

A: By the age of five, a child should be able to sit at a restaurant table for a reasonable period of time. The best way to encourage good restaurant manners is to practice at home. This means your child places his napkin in his lap, chews with his mouth closed, uses his utensils correctly, and remains seated until everyone is finished. Of course, all this takes practice, which is why I am such a big advocate of eating together as a family at least several times a week. Dinners don't have to be elaborate, but they do need to be eaten together. Even if dinner is macaroni and cheese, sit with your child at the table. When your child sees your good manners, he will be encouraged to improve his own.

Another effective way to encourage good restaurant manners is to take your kids to restaurants early in their lives. Be clear about expectations. Don't get lazy. When you tell your child that he cannot get up and wander around after his meal is finished, do not let your child get up and wander around.

When dining with toddlers, the best course of action is to take their needs into consideration. Keep crackers on hand in case the food takes longer than anticipated to arrive. Keep mealtimes short. Don't expect an eighteen-month-old to sit contently in a high chair for hours on end. Be realistic, but also be clear about behavior and consequences. If your toddler gets out of hand, be ready to take him out of the restaurant. Do not allow him to disturb other diners. If you are realistic and consistent in your expectations, you will soon have a child who is a joy to take to restaurants.

Q: **When a child needs a drink while visiting someone else's home, should he ask the host or his parent?**

A: Either a child or his parent may ask a host for a drink. Just make sure your child knows how to ask politely: "May I have a drink of water, please?"

Q: **When given a directive, should a child answer something back, such as, "Yes, Mom," "OK," or "Yes, sir"?**

A: Definitely! I call this becoming an "OK kid." This makes life easier for both parent and child. When your child responds with "OK, Mom," you know he has heard you, and it teaches him the importance of obedience.

191

Q: Should children be trained to keep their hands in their lap at a restaurant?

A: Adults as well as children should keep one hand in their laps when eating. When food is present, arms, elbows, and hands should not be on the table. However, before or after a meal, hands do not have to be in the lap. Just make sure your child's hands are not busy making a mess. (Unless we are talking about a toddler, and then a mess is pretty much a given!)

Q: When someone thanks your child, should she respond, "You're welcome," or give some kind of response even if nonverbal?

A: When someone thanks your child, she should respond with "You're welcome" and a smile.

Q: Is it proper for a child to "announce" who his best friend is in a social situation or around other kids?

A: Kids often proclaim their "friendship status" as a way of creating security and boundaries. Although this is common, help your child understand that part of being a good friend is being kind and considerate to everyone. Help him see how announcing his special friendship with one child will leave other children out and possibly hurt others' feelings. Part of growing up into a loving, caring person involves learning to take other people's feelings into consideration.

Q: Should a child give up her seat on a bus for an older person?

A: Children over the age of five should give up their seats for adults, especially the elderly, pregnant women, and parents with small children. This rule applies to travel on buses, subways, and when waiting in restaurants.

Q: Should a child ask to be excused from the dinner table, or is that an outdated custom?

A: Good manners never go out of style. When a child has finished eating, he should ask to be excused before leaving the table. It is also a nice idea to teach your child to thank the person who prepared the meal, by saying something like, "Thanks for dinner, Mom."

Q: My nieces and nephews stand on their couch and chairs when playing or watching TV. Naturally, when they visit my home, they do the same. I don't feel comfortable having them stand on my furniture. Am I out of line for feeling this way? If not, how should I handle this situation?

A: You are not at all out of line. Children must learn to respect adults, peers, themselves, and *things*. And that means no standing on couches, coffee tables, or other pieces of furniture. When your nieces and nephews visit, just kindly say that in your home you don't allow standing on furniture. Generally, kids only do what they can get away with. If you set limits in your home and stick to them, they will sit, not stand, on your furniture.

Q: We live where winters are long and cold. Not surprisingly, my children get antsy playing inside. Lately I've noticed that my kids as well as the neighbor kids sometimes run in the house. Is it proper manners for a child to run in the house?

A: Running inside the house is not only impolite, it is unsafe. For this reason, running should be reserved for outside play only. Even though your winters are long and cold, give your child ample time to play outdoors building snowmen, sledding, and playing games, or provide other ways for your kids to expend some of their God-given energy in a safe environment.

Q: What is the best way to invite only a few kids to your child's birthday party when they are all in the same class?

A: When inviting only a select number of children to any type of party, mail the invitations directly to the children's homes. Invitations should only be handed out at school if all classmates are invited. Make sure your child knows how important it is to avoid talking about his party when children who are not invited might overhear. Help him realize how hurtful it might be to a friend who did not receive an invitation. Tell him how proud you will be when he remembers to act with kindness toward others.

Q: How can I continually and gently remind my children to be polite without sounding like a broken record?

A: The answer is found within your question. You wisely used the words "continually" and "gently." Until your children have mastered a certain

193

etiquette skill, you will need to remind. However, when you remind gently, without shaming or embarrassing your children, they will eventually make your good manners their own.

In the meantime, to avoid repeating the same thing over and over, try asking your child questions. Before your child faces a social situation, ask something like, "When you meet Mrs. Smith today, what will you say?" "When we arrive at the restaurant, how will you behave?" "When you sit down to eat, what should you do with your napkin?" "How should you answer the phone this afternoon?" The use of questions allows your child to think about proper behavior and, best of all, keeps you from sounding like a broken record.

Q: How do I get my daughter to clean up after herself? She doesn't pick up her clothes, put shoes away, etc. I have become a nag! Help!

A: What parent hasn't faced this challenge? Whether it is teaching a preschooler to pick up toys or a teenager to pick up clothes, the battle can be intense.

When our son was three years old, I began the grueling task of teaching him to put his toys away on his own. At first this was a losing battle; he would begin but soon become distracted, at which point I would either become frustrated or resign myself to completing his job for him. Realizing that this pattern was doing neither of us any good, I came up with a solution that worked like a dream. I told Taylor that he could play with any toy he wished as long as he put it away at the end of the day. Any toy that was not put away before bedtime would be taken away and placed in a box to be kept for two weeks. At the close of the first day, after sufficient reminding, Taylor had put only a few of his coveted toys away. Calmly, I proceeded through his room and carefully placed all toys still on the floor in a box. At first this process didn't seem to bother him; he had plenty of other toys to keep him occupied. But by day four, the shortage of toys began to take its toll. Before the end of one week, three-year-old Taylor learned to pick up his toys and put them away all by himself.

The same method used for teaching Taylor to pick up his toys can be used to teach a child of any age to put away his or her things. The key is consistency and calmness. Your child may become emotional about "losing" her things, but you must not.

Another positive method to teach your child responsibility for her things is to provide a chore chart. Some kids just have difficulty remembering everything they are supposed to do. Seeing a list can be a helpful reminder for the forgetful child, and it can prevent you from becoming a nag.

Q: How do I get my two-year-old child to stop hitting? I have tried time-outs, making him hug the person, even spanking—nothing has worked. He still keeps on hitting. This is a nightmare! Please help!

A: One of the most difficult aspects of parenting is the fact that it often takes so long to see behavioral change in a child. This holds true whether your child is two or twelve. No doubt about it, parenting isn't for the faint of heart!

It's important to realize that *every* child goes through stages in which their behavior is less than ideal. Children aren't born knowing appropriate versus inappropriate behavior. It's our job to teach them. And quite often that takes time. Your two-year-old's hitting is not necessarily a reflection on your parenting. You should never be embarrassed that your child misbehaves; you should only be embarrassed if you fail to deal with his misbehavior.

The good news is that you *are* dealing with his misbehavior. The most effective method to get a child to stop any inappropriate behavior—hitting included—is negative reinforcement. Your child must feel the consequences of his misbehavior. When your child hits, remove him immediately. Tell him firmly that hitting hurts others and you will not allow hitting. Combine your negative reinforcement with positive reinforcement. Praise your child's kind behavior. He must learn that positive behavior generates positive attention.

Although it seems like your discipline hasn't worked thus far, give yourself and your child time. Remember, he's only two! If you remain firm, calm, and consistent, he *will* grow out of this stage.

Q: When other people hold my one-year-old, she often tries to put her fingers in their nose and mouth. This is very embarrassing, and I don't know what to do. Should I let the person handle it themselves, or should I interfere and gently move her hands away?

A: Touching, feeling, grabbing—these are ways the young child learns about her surroundings. Your one-year-old is simply exploring her world. There

195

is no need to be embarrassed by her behavior—at the age of one she has no idea her behavior is inappropriate. Most people will probably redirect your daughter's inquisitive hands on their own. If they don't, gently remove them yourself. In this way you will begin to teach your daughter appropriate behavior with others.

Q: **Is it considered polite manners to ask for seconds when eating at a friend's home?**

A: Asking for second helpings is a compliment to any chef! Just be sure that everyone has had a first helping and that there is enough for one or two others to also have seconds. For example, if you see only one piece of chicken left on a platter, you should not ask for seconds unless it is offered to you.

Q: **Is there a proper way to eat soup?**

A: When eating most soups, you should direct your soup spoon away from you. The reason is simple: so you don't splash soup on the table, or worse—on yourself. There are exceptions, however. Thick soups, chili, and stews may be eaten by directing your soup spoon toward you. Teach your child this catchy rhyme to help him remember the correct way to eat soup:

> As little ships go out to sea
> So my spoon goes away from me.

Q: **My teenagers love to talk on the phone, so they are usually the first to answer it as well. But if the call isn't for them, they can't seem to remember to write down messages. Do you have any suggestions?**

A: Make writing messages as easy as possible for all members of your family by keeping a pad of paper and a pen or pencil next to the phone. If your kids have easy access to the materials needed to take a message, your chances of receiving your messages are greatly increased.

However, since many of your kids' conversations probably take place as they wander throughout the house on a cordless phone, getting them to write down messages becomes a little trickier. You will need to make sure they understand that talking on the phone is a privilege and with that privilege comes responsibility. One of those responsibilities is showing respect to other family members by writing down messages. Your teens must understand that failing to take a message is more than just forgetfulness; it is inconsiderate and irresponsible.

While your kids learn to "remember" to write down your messages, try asking them, "Did I get any phone calls today?" at the day's end. This way you can ensure you get your messages even if your teens "forget" to write your messages down.

Q: What should my child do with her retainer while eating?

A: Your child should discreetly remove her retainer, place it in her retainer case or wrap it in a napkin, and place it in a purse, pocket, or other out of the way, but safe and easy to remember, place.

Q: Is there a proper way to eat fried chicken?

A: In casual settings such as a home or on a picnic, you may eat fried chicken with your hands. In a formal situation, you should cut pieces such as the breast or thigh. You may still use your fingers to eat the drumstick and wing.

Q: We have taught my five-year-old to say, "Excuse me," before interrupting her father or me when we are speaking with adults or on the phone, but lately she repeats "Excuse me" over and over until she gets our attention. Besides sounding rude, it's driving us nuts! Do you have any suggestions on how to deal with this problem?

A: Your situation is a common one. When a child wants our attention, she wants it *now*. She must learn to wait while at the same time understand that her need will be acknowledged by you. Saying, "Excuse me," is the polite way to interrupt adults when there is a break in the conversation flow. The problem arises when a young child doesn't understand the concept of a break in conversation. The result, as you have seen, is a child who says, "Excuse me," when you are in mid-sentence, or repeats the phrase over and over again.

To help combat this problem, teach your child to gently place her hand on your arm when she wants your attention. Tell her this will be her "secret, silent signal" that she needs your attention. In response, place your hand over her hand. This will be your "secret, silent signal" that you recognize her needs and will attend to her as soon as possible. One word

197

of caution: Don't wait too long until you respond to your child's need for you. Instead, say something like, "I'm sorry, Janet, my daughter has a question. Excuse me for a moment." Then attend to your child's need and resume your conversation.

Q: **We usually say a blessing before dinner in our home. Is it acceptable to say grace when we have dinner guests whose beliefs may differ from our own?**

A: How considerate you are for being concerned with making your guests feel comfortable in your home! Kindness and consideration are the hallmarks of proper etiquette.

In answer to your question, being invited to dine in someone else's home is a privilege and an honor. Part of what makes it special is experiencing how other families live. If saying a blessing before meals is part of your family's mealtime ritual, then it is perfectly acceptable to say a blessing when you have guests. To put guests at ease, you might say something like, "We usually say a prayer before our meals." Then proceed as usual.

Conclusion

Well done! You have completed the training. You are on your way to raising a confident, courteous child.

But the training doesn't end yet. Raising a loving, caring, well-mannered child isn't a fifty-yard dash. It's a marathon. But as every successful runner knows, what enables them to reach the finish line is not how fast they can run, but how well they have trained. Step by step, day by day, month by month they become more prepared to face the challenges of the race.

And so it is with your child. As you continue training your child in the basics contained in these pages, each step he takes will prepare him to face the challenges of life.

Raising kids is no simple task. It's not for the faint of heart or weak in spirit. But armed with wisdom, love, and God's grace, you *can* raise a well-mannered child.

You *can* tame your family zoo.

NOTES

Chapter 1: There Is Hope!

1. Deborah Wadsworth, Public Agenda Research Group, ABCNEWS. com, April 3, 2002.

2. "Who Says We're Rude?", RudeBusters, www.rudebusters.com/ who-says.htm.

3. Rasmussen Research, *Detroit News*, February 7, 2002.

Chapter 3: The Second Absolutely, Positively Essential Principle for Taming Your Family Zoo

1. James Dobson, *The New Dare to Discipline* (Carol Stream, IL: Tyndale House, 1996), 7.

2. Rebecca Prewitt, "Should Children Respect Adults?" www .schoolofabraham.com, August 2002.

Chapter 4: How to Raise a Brat

1. I first heard these ideas in 1989 on a tape called *Growing Kids God's Way* by Gary and Anne Marie Ezzo.

2. Ibid.

3. "Left Unsupervised: A Look at the Most Vulnerable Children," *Child Trends*, May 5, 2003, www.childtrends.org.

Chapter 7: Week 1: Everyday Manners for Everyday Monkeys

1. Dean-o, "Rad-Dude Attitude," *You Got It All*, BibleBeat Music/ASCAP, Mission Viejo, CA, 1997. Words and music by Dean-o. Lyrics used by permission.

2. Natalie Mead and Donna Jones, *Confidence & Courtesies Etiquette Course for Girls*, 1988.

Chapter 9: Week 3: Table Manners: It's Feeding Time at the Zoo

1. Blake Sperry Bowden and Jennie M. Zeisz, "Supper's On! Adolescent Adjustment and Frequency of Family Mealtimes," American Psychological Association 105th Annual Convention, Session 2220, August 16, 1997.

2. Washington State University School of Agriculture and Home Economics, "Families That Eat Together Not Only Eat Better, They Do Better," 2001.

3. Lynn Minton, "Dinner Is Our Peaceful Time," *Parade Magazine*, September 21, 2003.

4. Information on basic and informal table settings is taken from Peggy Post and Cindy Post Senning, Ed.D., *Emily Post's The Gift of Good Manners: A Parent's Guide to Raising Respectful, Kind, Considerate Children* (New York: HarperResource, 2002), 321–23.

5. Natalie Mead and Donna Jones, *Confidence & Courtesies Etiquette Course for Girls*, 1988.

Donna Jones holds a B.A. in interpersonal communications from UCLA and is the cofounder and owner of Confidence & Courtesies, an etiquette course for kids. She's been teaching children and teens manners since 1988 in both public and private schools and in department stores throughout California. Donna frequently speaks at women's retreats and MOPS events and is also a featured Bible teacher on the Doing Life Together DVD series. Donna and her family live in south Orange County, California.

Do you have a question you would like Donna to answer? If so, email her at donna-jones@cox.net.